113
04U8

D0412847

YORK NOTES

To be
If you wⁱ

HIGH WINDOWS

PHILIP LARKIN

NOTES BY STEVE EDDY

 Longman

 York Press

LIBRARY
NEWCASTLE COLLEGE
NEWCASTLE UPON TYNE
Class 821·914
BARCODE 02135779

The right of Steve Eddy to be identified as Author of this Work
has been asserted by him in accordance with the Copyright,
Designs and Patents Act 1988

YORK PRESS
322 Old Brompton Road, London SW5 9JH

PEARSON EDUCATION LIMITED
Edinburgh Gate, Harlow,
Essex CM20 2JE, United Kingdom
Associated companies, branches and representatives throughout the world

© Librairie du Liban *Publishers* 2007

Excerpts from 'To the Sea', 'Sympathy in White Major', 'The Trees', 'Livings I', 'Livings II',
'Livings III', 'Forget What Did', 'High Windows', 'Friday Night in the Royal Station Hotel', 'The
Old Fools', 'Going, Going', 'The Card-Players', 'The Building', 'Posterity', 'Dublinesque',
'Homage to a Government', 'This Be The Verse', 'How Distant', 'Sad Steps', 'Solar', 'Annus
Mirabilis', 'Show Saturday', *'Vers de Société'*, 'The Explosion', 'Money', and 'Cut Grass' from
High Windows by Philip Larkin. Copyright © 1974 by Philip Larkin. Reprinted by permission of
Farrar, Straus and Giroux, LLC; and Faber & Faber, Ltd, © The Philip Larkin Estate

All rights reserved. No part of this publication may be reproduced, stored
in a retrieval system, or transmitted in any form or by any means, electronic,
mechanical, photocopying, recording, or otherwise, without either the prior
written permission of the Publishers or a licence permitting restricted copying
in the United Kingdom issued by the Copyright Licensing Agency Ltd,
Saffron House, 6–10 Kirby Street, London EC1N 8TS

First published 2007

10 9 8 7 6 5 4 3 2 1

ISBN 978–1–4058–6182–3

Typeset by Pantek Arts Ltd, Maidstone, Kent
Printed in China

CONTENTS

PART THREE
CRITICAL APPROACHES

PART FOUR
CRITICAL HISTORY

PART FIVE
BACKGROUND

PART ONE

INTRODUCTION

HOW TO STUDY A POEM

Studying on your own requires self-discipline and a carefully thought-out work plan in order to be effective.

- Poetry is the most challenging kind of literary writing. In your first reading you may well not understand what the poem is about. Don't jump too swiftly to any conclusions about the poem's meaning.
- Read the poem many times, including out loud. After the second or third reading, write down any features you find interesting or unusual.
- What is the poem's tone of voice? What is the poem's mood?
- Does the poem have an argument? Is it descriptive?
- Is the poet writing in his or her own voice? Might he or she be using a **persona** or mask?
- Is there anything special about the kind of language the poet has chosen? Which words stand out? Why?
- What elements are repeated? Consider **alliteration, assonance,** rhyme, rhythm, **metaphor** and ideas.
- What might the poem's images suggest or **symbolise**?
- What might be significant about the way the poem is arranged in lines? Is there a regular pattern of lines? Does the grammar coincide with the ending of the lines or does it 'run over'? What is the effect of this?
- Do not consider the poem in isolation. Can you compare and contrast the poem with any other work by the same poet or with any other poem that deals with the same theme?
- What do you think the poem is about?
- Every argument you make about the poem must be backed up with details and quotations that explore its language and organisation.
- Always express your ideas in your own words.

These York Notes offer an introduction to *High Windows* and cannot substitute for close reading of the text and the study of secondary sources.

CHECK THE BOOK

See Stephen Metterson and Darren Jones, *Studying Poetry* (Hodder, 2000) for a good introduction.

READING *HIGH WINDOWS*

High Windows was published in 1974 and is Philip Larkin's final collection of poems. He wrote few significant poems after this, although he lived until 1985. Opinion on Larkin is divided, and this is perhaps more true of *High Windows* than for his earlier collections, especially *The Whitsun Weddings*. For many, he is England's unofficial National Poet, the spokesman for 'Middle England', affectionately describing English traditions and countryside and at other times displaying a typically British conservatism and pessimism. His poems are searching and profound, while at the same time being rooted in meticulous observation. Another great virtue of Larkin's poetry lies in his ability to mix the rhythms and cadences of ordinary speech with a highly original use of **imagery**.

For some critics, like Germaine Greer, Larkin is a good minor poet rather than a great one. Those who agree might cite the fact that Englishness – an important theme for Larkin – is not of global importance, and that this indicates a limited, parochial vision. Some might say his poems vary from the mundane to the obscure, and that his careful and precise observation, for example in 'Show Saturday', is rather pointless. Others may identify him with 'This Be The Verse' and dismiss him as shallow and vulgar, or at best preoccupied with his own psychological problems.

It cannot be denied that Larkin's passion for all things English would be limiting were it really his main theme. However, although he is identified with Englishness because of poems like 'The Whitsun Weddings' and, in *High Windows*, 'Going, Going', other themes, especially that of mortality, are more important in his poetry. Much of the time he is simply writing about what he knows. 'Show Saturday', for example, describes an English country fair, while 'To the Sea' focuses on the more recent tradition of the seaside visit. The social context in both of these is very English, but at a deeper level Larkin is writing about social ritual, community and the relationship between the individual and society. These are things which are of universal importance, especially when seen in relation to individual mortality.

CONTEXT

As a poet of 'Englishness', Larkin has occasionally been compared with John Betjeman (1906–84), the former Poet Laureate, although Betjeman was on the whole a much less serious poet. One of his classic poems is 'A Subaltern's Love Song', which begins: 'Miss J. Hunter Dunn, Miss J. Hunter Dunn,/ Furnish'd and burnish'd by Aldershot sun'.

It is interesting to consider Larkin's choice of subjects for his poems. Why should we be interested in the drab life of the agricultural salesman in 'Livings I', or the mundane detail of the village produce competition entries in 'Show Saturday', or even the crass dismissal of the poet by his own imagined biographer, 'Jake Balokowsky', in 'Posterity'? The answer is that there is much more to these subjects than meets the eye. The characterisation of the salesman in 'Livings I' is a beautifully understated study of a man whose dull life is underpinned by a deep longing, and who lives in a time of national, even global, uncertainty and change. Every detail in the poem is significant and worthy of examination.

Much the same is true of 'Show Saturday'. Here, although there is no central character, the individual show-goers are brought to life with warmth, originality and great economy. Take, for example, the 'children all saddle-swank' (50) and the 'husbands on leave from the garden,/ Watchful as weasels' (51–2). But the greater importance of the poem is in its exploration of community and seasonal continuity. Another poem which explores community, though in a more tragic context, is 'The Explosion'. This is a moving and strangely mystical poem.

Other poems in the collection are more obviously about universal themes. 'The Old Fools' and 'The Building' are about loss of choice, and individual mortality, but they are also poems about religion, or what Larkin sees as taking its place in a largely atheistic modern world. These poems, especially 'The Building', have a specifically English aspect in that the English are more in denial on the subject of mortality than, say, the Italians (or the Catholic Irish in 'Dublinesque'), but this in no way limits the importance of these poems.

Some of the poems are, in part, vulgar, and some can seem simplistic. However, Larkin's occasional use of the **vernacular** is a deliberate rejection of conservative poetic tradition, a breaking of the mould. Moreover, even a poem like 'This Be The Verse' is more subtle both in rhythm and **diction** than meets the eye. It also contains an example of the kind of rivetingly original **imagery** of which Larkin is capable: 'Man hands on misery to man./ It deepens like a coastal shelf' (9–10).

 CHECK THE NET

Larkin's reputation suffered from the publication of his letters, many of which expressed views that seemed mildly racist, sexist and right-wing. Some of these are quoted and commented on in articles on the website of the *New York Review of Books* (go to **www.nybooks.com** and search for Philip Larkin). However, it is worth bearing in mind that even the views expressed in these letters cannot be taken at face value, especially as we know that Larkin liked to shock and to entertain his friends. He would probably have had a difficult time in today's climate of political correctness.

CHECK THE NET

For information about the BBC documentary and drama about Larkin's life, go to the BBC homepage, **www.bbc.co.uk** and type 'Love and Death in Hull' into the search engine.

It is also a major characteristic of the poems in *High Windows* that many of them switch from the mundane to the sublime, and that this is reflected in the language. The title poem is the prime example; it moves from the sleazily casual first **stanza** to a vision of 'deep blue air, that shows/ Nothing, and is nowhere, and is endless' (20). Several other poems such as 'Sad Steps', 'Forget What Did' and 'Money' have this kind of breathtaking 'twist in the tail'.

An interesting feature of *High Windows* is its use of narrative voices, or **personae**. This does not make the poems difficult to read – in fact it may make it easier to relate to them. However, it is often impossible to be sure how far Larkin is adopting a persona, or to what extent he is addressing us directly. For some commentators the answer is to treat every poem which seems to present an opinion or address us in the first person as being in the voice of a fictional **narrator**, rather than expressing Larkin's own views. This is preferable to regarding every view as Larkin's own, but there are times when it seems ridiculous. We could, for example, say that 'the narrator' of 'The Old Fools' is angry about human aging and mortality, but Larkin, when faced with criticism of the poem on its publication, made no attempt to hide behind a persona. He frankly admitted that the anger was his own.

Similarly, 'Going, Going' appears to express (perhaps too freely) Larkin's attitude to the decline of his ideal England. 'To the Sea' reveals Larkin's thoughts and feelings about seaside visits – including his own childhood memories and a mention of how his parents met. 'Money' also appears to express Larkin's attitude to materialism, even if we cannot take it as his last word on the subject.

At other times, Larkin is clearly revealing to us an aspect of his own personality. In 'Posterity', he shows both his contempt for some aspects of the academic world, and a certain sympathy for 'Jake Balokowsky', who (as Larkin later observed) has quite a lot in common with him. He too has to work for a living when he would rather be doing something else. 'Homage to a Government' expresses a rather naïve political view about which Larkin was inclined to be defensive when interviewed. 'Livings II' is narrated by an enigmatic (and perhaps slightly deranged) lighthouse keeper whose intensely poetic language and avoidance of the outside world expresses some aspects of Larkin's character. It would be a mistake, however, to see him as 'Larkin in disguise'. Similarly, 'Annus Mirabilis' is narrated by a mournfully pathetic character for whom the sexual liberation of the 1960s came just too late. This expresses the awkwardness with women that was part of Larkin's character, especially in his youth. We cannot simply say that this persona is Larkin, however, particularly since we now know that he had a number of relationships with women.

If some poems in *High Windows* seem deceptively simple, others seem quite obscure – as some critics (including Clive James) have commented. 'Livings II' has been called obscure, and it does have one or two difficult lines (for example line 14, 'Radio rubs its legs'), but despite its rich imagery, it is not hard to understand once we grasp that it is about a lighthouse keeper. What we make of his desire to keep the outside world at bay is another matter, but then no poem should be regarded purely as an exercise in translation. Similarly, '*Vers de Société*' has been called difficult (which is one reason why it has been made the subject of an extended commentary in this guide), but it is how we view the significance of what is described that is challenging, rather than the basic sense of what is being said.

We should not be fooled into taking the apparently simple poems at face value, nor daunted by those which at first seem difficult. Larkin has such an ability to make verse sound natural that we should make a point of looking for the features that distinguish it as verse; for example, his subtle use of **metre**, rhythm and rhyme, his telling imagery, and his use of **symbolism**. His rhymes, especially, sound so natural that they can easily be missed, and his diction tends to be conversational – not obviously poetic.

CHECK THE BOOK

For further comments on the obscurity of some poems in *High Windows*, see Clive James, 'Don Juan in Hull: Philip Larkin', in *At the Pillars of Hercules* (Faber, 1979).

PART TWO

THE TEXT

NOTE ON THE TEXT

High Windows was first published by Faber and Faber in hardback in 1974, and in paperback in 1979. The order of the poems is the same in both these editions, but differs in Larkin's *Collected Poems* (Faber, first published 1988). The 1979 paperback edition has been used in the preparation of these Notes.

DETAILED COMMENTARIES

TO THE SEA

- Larkin rejoices in the continuation of the traditional ritual of seaside visits.
- He reflects on his own childhood visits to the seaside and on the social value of this ritual.

CONTEXT

Larkin's depiction of the beach in stanza 1 bears comparison to many paintings depicting beach and bathing scenes, such as 'The Beach at Trouville' by Claude Monet (1870), 'Bathers at Asnière' by George Seurat (1884), and 'South Beach' by John Sloan (1907).

In this opening poem, Larkin paints an affectionate – even nostalgic – picture of an English holiday beach and celebrates this peculiarly English expression of humanity. It is a world that seems to exist in isolation, a place of escape into what is, after all, an illusory timelessness. There is in the final **stanza** a sense of time passing, but only to make way for another day. This stanza also draws a tentative moral – that these ordinary people are somehow an example in their sense of community and social duty.

The poem previews a number of themes developed in more depth later, especially in 'Show Saturday'. There is the portrayal of Englishness and its sense of social responsibility. We also glimpse youth and age, in stanza 2: 'uncertain children' (14) and 'The rigid old' (16), with death waiting in the wings. We see Larkin's recurring slide between pleasurable solitude and loneliness (stanza 3). And finally, there is the phenomenon of the seaside visit as a ritual that helps to fill the gap left by religion.

COMMENTARY

From the first line we are given a sense that this world is separate – which is perhaps why it is apparently untouched by time. The 'low wall' (1) is a boundary between the real world and this partially idealised one. Even the phrase 'something known long before' (3) suggests something that has always existed. Yet 'miniature gaiety' (4) indicates a limited scope, despite the colourful list of its components: 'Steep beach, blue water, towels, red bathing caps' (6).

Everything here is faintly idealised, from the politely 'hushed' waves repeatedly collapsing in a reassuringly predictable way, to the 'warm yellow sand' (7–8). The 'white steamer' seems to the distant viewer to be stationary, 'stuck in the afternoon' (9), like this artificially timeless scene.

At the start of stanza 2, Larkin exclaims in a characteristic way (as he does, for example, in the final line of 'The Card-Players'), rejoicing in the survival of this seaside scene. The pleasures he mentions are simple ones, though they include listening to transistor radios – the 1960s equivalent of the i-Pod. The children seem charming, 'frilled in white' (14), and, as city-dwellers, unaccustomed to the space ('enormous air' [15]). In the long sentence beginning 'To lie . . .' and continuing into the next stanza (11–22), we see unspecified visitors leading the children and pushing the old in wheelchairs – expressions of kindness or social duty that Larkin applauds at the end of the poem.

In the continuation of the sentence in stanza 3, Larkin briefly introduces himself into the poem, recalling himself as a child, happy to have got away from his parents to indulge in a very English pastime – searching for cigarette cards depicting famous cricketers. He also alludes to his own parents' first meeting, listening to a performer dismissively summed up by Larkin with the word 'quack' (22). (See 'Show Saturday' for another use of this word).

Having not been to the seaside for some time, he is 'Strange to it now' (23), but all the details he describes are unchanged: sky, the water, pebbles – rhyming neatly with the high-pitched 'trebles' (25) of the bathers who shriek at the cold water. The 'cheap cigars' (26)

CHECK THE BOOK

One poet who influenced Larkin, and also alludes to being happy alone as Larkin does in this poem, is Edward Thomas (1878–1917). See his 'It Rains', in *Collected Poems* (Faber, 1979), where he writes: 'Sad, too, to think that never, never again,/ Unless alone, so happy shall I walk/ In the rain.'

suggest lower-middle-class fathers treating themselves, while the chocolate papers perhaps relate to their children, and the tea-leaves (in the days before tea bags were invented and tea was mostly made by women!) their wives.

In the final stanza, time has passed and the white steamer has finally gone. Light, for Larkin, so often symbolises some form of hope or transcendence of the material world. Here we see that the sunlight has turned 'milky', like 'breathed-on glass' (30–1), the image of milk perhaps connecting to cups of tea and the misted glass hinting at children amusing themselves in the car on the way home. Perhaps this change in the light hints at a fading of the illusion of timelessness.

The last part of the poem is more challenging. Larkin seems to be saying that the only bad thing about perfect weather is that we cannot equal it. If so, these day trippers are at their best as human beings. Their clumsy undressing reflects a rather inept Englishness that Larkin often celebrates. But they come almost as a religious ritual every year: the visit is 'half an annual pleasure, half a rite' (18). They seem inept, too, in the way they teach their children, but they mean well and they do their duty towards the old 'as they ought' (36).

> **? QUESTION**
> At the end of 'To the Sea' Larkin seems to say that in the absence of any higher purpose, observing communal rituals is at least as worthwhile as any other form of behaviour. Do you see this as a positive social comment, or is Larkin saying that life is so meaningless that ritual is all we have?

> **GLOSSARY**
> 20 **Famous Cricketers** 'Caricatures of Famous Cricketers' (Australian and English Test cricketers 1900–26). These collectable cards were issued, in packets of cigarettes made by R. & J. Hill Sunripe Cigarettes, in 1926, when Larkin was four years old
> 22 **quack** a charlatan

SYMPATHY IN WHITE MAJOR

- The speaker of the poem pours a gin and tonic.
- The speaker raises his glass and drinks a toast to himself.

Larkin, speaking either for himself or in the voice of a **narrator**, describes pouring a gin and tonic and drinking a toast to himself, as if speaking aloud his own obituary, commenting **ironically** on his achievements. The poet seems to reflect somewhat **ambiguously** on his professional efforts and their limited success. In the final **stanza**, in a string of ironic platitudes, he extols his own virtues in a deliberately implausible way, before pulling the rug from under his own feet, with a postscript that quietly invalidates them.

COMMENTARY

Clive James, in a review in the magazine *Encounter* (June 1974), commented on the obscurity of this poem: 'While wanting to be just the reverse, Larkin can on occasion be a difficult poet.' In terms of vocabulary and **syntax** the poem is deceptively simple. Nor is there complex **imagery** to unravel – there is no imagery at all, unless you count the **clichés** 'Straight as a die . . . A brick, a trump' (18–19). Moreover, the deliberately straightforward language is reinforced by a simple **iambic metre** and a regular rhyme scheme. The difficulty lies in what significance we should read into the poet, or the narrator, toasting himself in this way – and in particular what we should make of the final line.

The poem becomes clearer if we accept Barbara Everett's very convincing case for it providing evidence of Larkin having read French **Symbolist** poetry (*Poets in their Time*, Faber, 1986). According to her, the title parodies a poem of 1850 by Théophile Gautier, '*Symphonie en blanc majeure*' (Symphony in White Major), which describes the whiteness of a female swan. In the 1860s a French art critic used Gautier's phrase to describe a painting by Laurence Whistler of a woman in white, 'White Girl'. Whistler responded by renaming his painting '*Symphonie in White No. 1*', and went on to paint a sequel depicting a woman in white half-looking at herself in a mirror. The poet Swinburne wrote a poem based on this called 'Before the Mirror'. These works arguably explore the artist contemplating himself and his art – which is what Larkin is doing in this poem. Everett suggests that Larkin was influenced by the French poet Mallarmé, who in 1893 wrote a poem called '*Salut*' ('Cheers'), which he first delivered with a champagne glass in his hand. In this poem, poetry is compared to champagne bubbles – 'Nothing, this foam, virgin verse', in a way which Larkin

CHECK THE NET

Images of Whistler's two 'Symphony in White' paintings can be seen on the website **www.ibiblio.org** together with background information about them. 'No. 1' is in the National Gallery of Art, Washington, USA; 'No. 2' is in Tate Britain, London. Go to the address above and then search for 'Whistler'.

CONTEXT

Théophile Gautier (1811–72) was a French poet, novelist and critic. He was a champion of art for art's sake – which is relevant to Larkin's apparent exploration of the value of poetic endeavour in 'Sympathy in White Major'.

CONTEXT

Stéphane Mallarmé (1842–98), generally regarded as a founder of modern European poetry, was in turn influenced by the **Symbolist** poet Charles Baudelaire (1821–67).

may be recalling in the 'foaming gulps' (5) of the tonic which he allows to 'void' (4) (or, in other words, empty – relating to Mallarmé's 'Nothing'). The whiteness of Larkin's **narrator** relates to the whiteness of the drink and of the 'virgin verse'.

If Everett is correct, then 'Sympathy in White Major' can be seen as the poet self-consciously reflecting on the value of his poetry. He comments in an **ironically** self-disparaging way on his own virtue, or 'whiteness' as a poet dedicated to art for its own sake, and resurrects the 'lost displays' (12) – perhaps those of poets gone before. **Stanza** 1 focuses in great detail on the gin and tonic. We hear the chime of the ice cubes and see the foam and hear the 'gulps' (5) of the tonic being poured. The poet seems to enjoy this process, and perhaps to find sympathy or consolation in it. The detailing of the exact method suggests that he is indulging himself by pouring a drink exactly as he likes it, as if in reward for having *'devoted his life to others'* (8). However, this phrase, italicised like the other heavily ironic lines in stanza 3, cannot be taken literally. Larkin seems to be almost sneering at his own poetic achievement, as if saying that actually it has not done much for others at all.

In stanza 2 the poet compares himself, again ironically, with less altruistic people who exploited others. There is a sense of **bathos** in the simple admission 'It didn't work for them or me' (13) which deflates the grand endeavour of the 'lost displays' (12). Even the slight acknowledgement of achievement is undermined by the lines:

? **QUESTION**
The phrase 'the fuss' (15) makes the aim seem prosaic, while 'Or so we thought' (15) suggests that even this belief was deluded, and missing the goal together seems little better than missing it separately. What do you personally think Larkin means here? And is he being unnecessarily obscure?

> But all concerned were nearer thus
> (Or so we thought) to all the fuss
> Than if we'd missed it separately. (14–16)

The final stanza reels off a procession of **clichés** of the sort that might be spoken by casually well-meaning friends after a death, standing with drinks ready for the toast: *'Here's to the whitest man I know'* (23). This line is **ambiguous**. It means white in the sense of pure and virtuous (as in Whistler's paintings), yet it contains a hint of hypocrisy too, as when someone is described as 'whiter than white' – i.e. only appearing to be virtuous. There may even be a racial element – white in the sense of a white man in **post-colonial** Britain. The final line is undramatic in the extreme, as if merely an incidental comment, yet it gives the poem a twist which shrugs off all the clichés that have gone before.

GLOSSARY

3	**goes**	shots (i.e. the speaker pours a triple gin and tonic)
18	**die**	a straight-edged metal block used in manufacturing to shape soft materials
19	**brick**	a reliable person
	trump	a **colloquial** phrase meaning a reliable or admirable person; literally a high-ranking card in a card game
	sport	an old-fashioned colloquial term for someone prepared to abide by the rules of a game; more loosely, someone who is good company

---

THE TREES

- Larkin contemplates the trees coming into leaf as a symbol of nature's cycle of life and death.

In this short poem about change, aging and renewal, Larkin's feelings seem to be ambivalent: the trees appear to be renewed but do eventually die. Nevertheless they urge the poet to embrace life afresh.

COMMENTARY

The language of this poem is simple, the rhyme scheme and **metre** unchallenging. However, the attitude expressed is more complex. The trees are **personified, metaphors** for change and renewal. Their being 'Like something almost being said' (2) makes them similar to the poem itself: its message is not explicit. Larkin sways between hope and pessimism. The positivity of 'relax and spread' (3) is balanced by the leaves being 'a kind of grief' (4) – perhaps because this positive growth cannot last.

In **stanza** 2 Larkin explores the phenomenon with a question, but concludes that the trees only appear to renew themselves: the rings laid down in their grain (circles within the trunk – one for each year – that we see when a tree is felled) reveal that they, too, are aging and will eventually die.

QUESTION
What, if anything, do you think the trees are 'almost' saying?

CONTEXT

'The Trees' may be compared with a short poem by Robert Frost (1864–1963), 'Nothing Gold Can Stay' which also uses the seasonal changes in trees as a **symbol** of more general change, and of mortality.

In **stanza** 3 Larkin supplants his intellectual analysis with his emotional response to the trees. They seem strong, active and masculine: 'unresting castles' which 'thresh/ in fullgrown thickness' (9–10). The image suggests both the outline of the trees, like castle turrets, and their resilience. Castles could also suggest isolation – felt by the poet and projected onto the trees: the hotel in 'Friday Night in the Royal Station Hotel' is described as fort-like in its isolation.

Larkin finishes with the rather fanciful image of the trees announcing the death of the old year and urging him to start anew. The **sibilance** of 'seem to say' (11) and the **onomatopoeic** repetition of 'afresh' (12) vigorously reproduces their leafy rustling. However, given the 'grief' (4) of stanza 1 and the proven mortality of the trees, we can assume that Larkin does not find it easy to act on their advice.

FORGET WHAT DID

- The poet describes himself giving up writing a diary in order to numb the pain that it brings.
- He wishes for the blank pages to be filled with comforting natural events.

CONTEXT

Andrew Motion, in his biography, says that Larkin began 'Forget What Did' at the end of January 1967, and that it describes how Larkin stopped writing his diary earlier that month, because his feelings about his mistress Maeve Brennan's new admirer were too painful to record.

Setting aside the biographical nature of this poem, it describes a man deciding to avoid the heightened pain of recording his own suffering in a diary. He considers replacing the mundane events of his own life with celestial and natural events.

COMMENTARY

This is a rather bleak poem, which, while describing an attempt to avoid pain, actually evokes it quite poignantly. The rather faltering **metre** is composed of **dactyls** (as in the first line), **trochees** (as in the second) and **spondees** (as in 'As bleakened waking'). By avoiding the more common and easily flowing **iambic** rhythm found, for example, in the first stanza of 'The Trees', Larkin produces a slow-moving, introspective mood.

The suddenness of the opening word is emphasised by its
alliteration with 'stun' (2) and 'starting' (3). The most emotive
word here is 'stun', suggesting as it does that the poet wanted to
curtail painful memories, even if it took a fairly brutal cure to do it.
The word 'cicatrized' (4) in the next stanza makes the pain more
acute. Memories, evidently, made all his waking moments bleak.
The 'blank starting' (3) was supposed to be a fresh start, but the
word 'blank' is bleak, and moreover there is the second meaning of
'starting': being made to jump up in shock.

The third stanza simply states the poet's desire to bury the past, as
something to recollect from a distance, almost invisible, 'Like the
wars and winters' (10) of a forgotten childhood. It is interesting
that Larkin uses the image of windows here, linked with opacity
(non-transparency), as this poem appears opposite 'High Windows'
in the collection as published.

The mood shifts somewhat in the last two stanzas, as Larkin
appears to seek consolation in soothing natural events and images.
However, this consolation seems a little **ambiguous**. Larkin is not
sure that the 'empty pages' (13) should ever be filled. If they are,
the 'Celestial recurrences' (16) detailed seem impersonal, even
though the word 'Celestial' suggests something beyond petty
human suffering. If this is indeed a consolation, it is one akin to
that offered by the stellar constellations at the end of 'Livings III',
putting petty personal circumstances in perspective. However,
although the word 'recurrences' seems optimistic in that it points to
a continuation of life, the final line refers to an ending –
presumably the migration of birds in the autumn, signalling the
onset of winter.

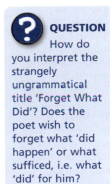

QUESTION
How do
you interpret the
strangely
ungrammatical
title 'Forget What
Did'? Does the
poet wish to
forget what 'did
happen' or what
sufficed, i.e. what
'did' for him?

GLOSSARY		
4	cicatrized	scarred
16	celestial	relating to the sky, or to heavenly bodies

CONTEXT

Barbara Everett (*Poets in their Time*, Faber, 1986) argues that 'High Windows' is influenced by Mallarmé's poem '*Les fenêtres*'. In this poem, an old man dying in hospital looks longingly at the azure blue sky beyond the windows. She says that this poem itself is influenced by two prose poems by Baudelaire. Andrew Motion, too, in his biography of Larkin comments that 'High Windows' is 'subtly influenced' by the **Symbolist** writers he later decried – and 'the Symbolist-influenced ones he also scorned, notably Eliot'.

  CHECK THE NET

For an online French language version of Mallarmé's poem '*Les fenêtres*', go to **www.poesie.webnet. fr** and type 'Mallarme' into the search engine under 'Auteur'.

HIGH WINDOWS

- Larkin comments on the sexual freedom of modern times and questions whether the generation before his own saw him in a similar way.

- He breaks away to a vision of the sublime inspired by the view through high windows.

In the title poem – an important one which strikes a keynote for the collection as a whole – Larkin creates a **persona** reflecting on modern-day sexual liberty in a characteristically **ambiguous** and ambivalent way. His deliberately banal tone reflects this ambivalence. Putting his own feelings in perspective, he speculates about whether those who came before him were similarly jealous of him, specifically for his generation's escape from the confines of religious orthodoxy. In the final **stanza** he is transported to a vision of the sublime that transcends religious dogma and defies definition.

COMMENTARY

This is a poem full of contradictions. It does most clearly what several other poems in the collection do to a lesser extent. It begins in a relatively banal way and surprises us with a move towards something transcendent in the last few lines. The poems on either side of this one, 'Forget What Did' and 'Friday Night in the Royal Station Hotel', also follow this pattern; so does 'Sad Steps', which transcends personal disappointments to find a sort of consolation in the lives of others. However, 'High Windows' is the only one which specifically addresses religion versus spirituality. Andrew Motion, in *Philip Larkin: A Writer's Life*, notes his contrasting voices, especially in 'High Windows':

> One of the most characteristic features of his later poems is the way they introduce a demotic, street-wise language . . . to a more rarefied and poetic one.

The first part of the poem can be seen both as Larkin himself speaking directly to us, and as an **ironic** persona that he has created. Either way, the sentiments cannot be taken literally. There is a hardness in the **alliteration** of the 'u' sounds in lines 1 and 2, which, together with the studied casualness of the language and the harshly unromantic details of contraception, betray a certain bitterness mingled with distaste. As in 'Annus Mirabilis', Larkin's view of sex is complicated: he appears to feel that he has missed out on sex, and yet he is rather disgusted by it. Certainly the lines 'I know this is paradise/ Everyone old has dreamed of all their lives' (4–5) is heavily ironic. His banal description of sexual freedom is at odds with the idea of 'paradise' and the dismissal of 'Bonds and gestures' (6) – commitment and affection – seems irresponsible. Sex, in effect, is being trivialised. The effect is exaggerated by the slightly absurd image of the 'outdated combine harvester' (7) – in which Andrew Motion sees a buried hint that no one ever really 'gets their oats'.

The idea of 'everyone young going down the long slide/ To happiness, endlessly' (8–9) is not credible. At the same time, this image is itself ambiguous: the slide comes from a playground, suggesting irresponsibility or at least childishness, but it also hints at moral decline, as well as sexual penetration. One wonders, too, if the clear-cut distinction between young and old is actually how Larkin sees things, or whether this, also, is meant **ironically**.

A second persona is created in the italicised section containing the imagined expectation of Larkin's own predecessors. This new voice enviously, and **colloquially**, anticipates the religious freedom of Larkin's generation, the envy showing especially in '*Like free bloody birds*' (16). Even here, although the focus is on religion, the '*sweating in the dark*' (12) suggests sexual guilt.

At the end of the fourth stanza there is an abrupt change of tone from the mundane to the sublime. Larkin is suddenly struck by a thought which, paradoxically, is 'Rather than words' (17), but is nevertheless expressed in words. But even this 'thought of high windows' (17) is ambiguous. The windows offer a view of something beyond the mundane world, yet this is only possible because they are high, revealing only sky, not the world at ground level. At the same time, their height may reflect the elevation of the vision which they inspire. They are 'sun-comprehending' (18) (which links this poem to 'Solar'), suggesting that their glass reveals the sublime, yet this vision of the sublime is a negative one:

CHECK THE BOOK

Professor Ray Billington's book *Religion without God* (Routledge, 2001) is a very readable philosophical exploration of the possibility of a spirituality unfettered by religious dogma.

CHECK THE BOOK

William Golding's novel *The Spire* (1964) presents a similar image of unworldly spirituality to that of 'High Windows' when the main character, Dean Jocelin, glimpses blue sky through a hole in the roof of his cathedral.

'Nothing, and . . . nowhere' (20). If it achieves the sublime, it does so by transcending the world of things and places.

GLOSSARY		
3	**pills** contraceptive pills	
4	**diaphragm** a contraceptive device worn by women	
18	**sun-comprehending** here this seems to mean transparent; letting light through	

FRIDAY NIGHT IN THE ROYAL STATION HOTEL

- Larkin describes the scene inside an almost deserted hotel.

In this poem, which is loosely speaking a **sonnet**, Larkin describes an entirely man-made yet deserted setting. The fact that at other times it is full of people makes it seem particularly empty and lonely now. Unlike many of Larkin's poems, there is no **narrative**, no **persona** behind the lines, and no cast of characters. The emphasis is entirely on atmosphere.

COMMENTARY

'Friday Night in the Royal Station Hotel' is unusual in that it describes a setting in detail, but almost completely without human occupants. The furnishings and signs of recent occupation only highlight the absence of humanity. The effect is to create an atmosphere of looming loneliness and emptiness.

As in several poems in *High Windows* (notably 'Livings II'), light plays an important role. In fact, 'Light' (1) is the first word of the poem. Larkin uses a loose **oxymoron** to describe the way in which it 'spreads darkly downwards' (1), the heavy-sounding **alliteration** adding to the contradiction: dark, heavy light. The second line adds to this: 'Clusters of lights' (2) brings to mind clusters of people, but the light only illuminates their absence, in the form of 'empty chairs' (2). The mixed colouring of the chairs is an odd detail, perhaps indicating a slight shabbiness in the hotel.

Just as the chairs are given a sort of blank personality in that they 'face each other' (3), so the dining-room is given a voice: it 'declares' (4). The alliteration in 'larger loneliness' (5) exaggerates the sombre mood, the 'knives and glass' (5) are hard and slightly threatening, and the silence is palpable – 'like carpet' (6). The glimpsed porter only adds to this mood; even his paper is unsold because there is no one there to buy it. There is a sense of time passing, as in 'To the Sea' or 'Show Saturday', but here nothing happens. Activity has ceased with the departure of the salesmen: no one has even emptied the ashtrays!

The second **stanza** moves from the conference rooms to the corridors upstairs, off which are the guest rooms. The corridors are shoeless because the rooms are unoccupied: no one has left shoes outside their door to be cleaned. The lights still 'burn' (10), emphasising the emptiness like the lights earlier in the poem.

Larkin uses **enjambment** to place the emotive 'Isolated' at the start of a line (11). The hotel's fortress-like isolation makes it a suitable place in which to be exiled – cut off from society, homeless. The mood created is such that when we reach the rather mystifying italicised last line, the phrase *'Now/ Night comes on'* (14) suggests imminent death, while *'Waves fold behind villages'* (14) implies the threat of an elemental world beyond the fortress of the hotel. If the hotel of the title is the one close to where Larkin lived in Hull, a town on the east coast of England, the line could refer to the sea nearby, which could pose a possible threat to the low-lying villages. Less prosaically, we are left with a strange sense of something ominous and impersonal.

This poem relates to 'Livings II' (see **Extended commentaries**), which is narrated by a lighthouse keeper. Both the lighthouse and the hotel in 'Friday Night in the Royal Station Hotel' are isolated. In the latter the light adds to the sense of loneliness, whereas in 'Livings II' it helps to preserve the **narrator**'s isolation. In both poems the outside world presents a threat, partly suggested by images of the sea.

 CHECK THE NET

The paintings of the American artist Edward Hopper (1882–1968) often evoke some of the same sense of lonely displacement found in 'Friday Night in the Royal Station Hotel', especially the painting which is probably his most famous, 'Nighthawks' (1942), which pictures people in an almost deserted bar late at night. Hopper's use of light and shadow also has something in common with Larkin's use of 'dark light'. To see this painting online, go to **www.artchive.com** and type 'Hopper' into the search engine.

QUESTION

What is your personal interpretation of the last sentence of 'Friday Night in the Royal Station Hotel'?

THE OLD FOOLS

- Larkin considers the incapacitated elderly and what they must think.

- He gives a view on what happens at death and before birth.

- He speculates as to what it must be like to be old.

CONTEXT

As Britain declared war in August 1914, many recruits were 'sloping arms' – shouldering their rifles – by September 1914. This may be why Larkin names this month in 'The Old Fools'. When he wrote the poem in 1973, the young recruits of 1914 were approaching their eighties. Larkin's own mother, Eva, was 87, and was already in decline in a nursing home, where Larkin, visiting her, would have seen for himself the things he describes in the poem. Eva eventually died aged 91.

In this emotionally challenging poem, Larkin describes the mental confusion, incontinence and physical disability of the elderly with more distaste than sympathy – though perhaps because he is anticipating the same fate himself, as the last line suggests. However, this is also a poem about death, which for Larkin is 'oblivion' (15), and one which by implication celebrates life.

COMMENTARY

Even the title of this poem is controversial. One might expect Larkin, as someone who is in some ways a conservative figure, to show some respect for the elderly. Failing that, bearing in mind that in 'To the Sea' he writes of 'helping the old, too, as they ought' (36), one might expect him to be sympathetic to their plight. Instead, his language shows disgust: 'drools . . . pissing yourself . . . Ash hair, toad hands, prune face' (3–4, 23). He describes their plight as a 'hideous inverted childhood' (47). Some of the lines even seem mocking – the title itself, and its repetition in the body of the poem, the **rhetorical question** 'Do they somehow suppose/ It's more grown-up when your mouth hangs open and drools . . .' (3), the harshness of 'crippled or tight' (9). Even the arresting 'Why aren't they screaming?' (12) is preceded by the detached 'it's strange' (11). In the first **stanza**, only the imagined recollections of the elderly humanise and soften this mood:

> . . . to when they danced all night,
> Or went to their wedding, or sloped arms some
> September? (6–7)

After the poem was published in the magazine *The Listener*, in the early months of 1973, Larkin responded to criticism of it for being hard-hearted:

It is indeed an angry poem, but the anger is ambivalent: there is anger at the humiliation of age . . . but there is also an anger at the old for reminding us of death, and anger is especially common today when most of us believe that death ends everything. (Letter to M. Shirley, 7 February 1973, reprinted in Andrew Motion, *Philip Larkin: A Writer's Life*)

The switch to metaphysical speculation in the second stanza is abrupt. The simplicity of the language makes Larkin's view of death matter-of-fact: we are reduced to 'the bits that were you' (13), and the rhyming of 'you' and 'oblivion, true' (15) seems deliberately trite, as if to make light, **ironically**, of our lives being reduced to nothing in this way. However, Larkin then surprises us with his view of a pre-life state, which makes human life seems uniquely meaningful and wonderful:

> . . . all the time merging with a unique endeavour
> To bring to bloom the million-petalled flower
> Of being here. (17–19)

The next thought – 'Next time you can't pretend/ There'll be anything else' (19–20) makes it clear that Larkin does not believe in reincarnation. And the confusion of the elderly heralds the coming oblivion. Significantly, too, for them the power of choice is gone: Larkin associates life with choice, and therefore a loss of choice is for him a diminution of life.

In the third stanza, Larkin does make a serious attempt to empathise with the old, employing an image of light (as he so often does), in speculating that being old might be 'having lighted rooms/ Inside your head' (25–6), occupied by people who are familiar but not quite identifiable. This is a sensitive and delicate view of the possible mental state of those who are beginning to lose touch with reality. As in 'Friday Night at the Royal Station Hotel', chairs, presumably empty, stand as a symbol of loneliness, like the bush at the window. The 'sun's/ Faint friendliness on the wall' (32–3) is so slight a comfort as to emphasise the overall bleakness of life for the elderly.

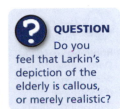

QUESTION
Do you feel that Larkin's depiction of the elderly is callous, or merely realistic?

CHECK THE BOOK
Look at Dylan Thomas' famous poem, 'Do not go gentle into that good night', which also explores themes of death and aging. Thomas argues 'Old age should burn and rave at close of day', and not accept death meekly. See *Collected Poems, 1934–1953* (Everyman, 2000).

CHECK THE BOOK

Robin Spice, *Living With Dementia – A Son's Story* (Exposure Publishing, 2006), gives an account of his own experience of his mother gradually developing Alzheimer's disease. Sufferers experience a gradual loss of memory and recognition of previously familiar things, as described in 'The Old Fools'.

Larkin strains to explain to himself, and us, the 'air of baffled absence' (37) surrounding the old, which he attributes to their desire to live in the past, although still forced to be here in the present. His image of the rooms inside the old people's heads growing farther away is like the receding hospital rooms in 'The Building', each room being nearer to death. Andrew Motion, in fact, identifies these two poems as companions to each other (see *Philip Larkin: A Writer's Life*, p. 426).

Perhaps the most arresting image is 'Extinction's alp' (41). Extinction somehow seems more extreme than death – if that is possible – and the use of the singular (one normally thinks of the Alps – plural) makes death seem all the more unavoidable and lonely. It is death's very proximity that makes it hard to see clearly.

Old age, then, in this poem is seen with horror, appalling in its loss of choice, its indignity, and its return to childhood dependence, but ultimately in its announcement of the final oblivion. The poem may seem unsympathetic, but this may be because Larkin is largely anticipating his own decline. As he comments in the last line, in answer to his final question, 'We shall find out' (48). This seems rather an anti-climax.

GLOSSARY		
7	**sloped arms**	shouldered a rifle on military parade
9	**tight**	drunk

GOING, GOING

- Larkin writes of his concern that the English countryside as he knows it will have disappeared within his lifetime.

This poem expresses Larkin's more conservative and pessimistic outlook, as well as his love for what he sees as quintessentially English. He bemoans the loss of old buildings and the erection of new and ugly ones on greenfield sites, as well as increasing pollution. He blames the materialism of ordinary people and the greed of businessmen, and predicts that soon England will have become one big slum. The poem was commissioned by the Countess of Dartmouth, head of a government committee reporting on 'The Human Habitat'. The committee objected to the attack on big business made in **stanza 5**, which was therefore omitted when the poem was published in the committee's report. The stanza was restored in *High Windows*.

COMMENTARY

This poem is often seen as typical of Larkin, expressing his love of all things English and his fear that they will be swept away by materialistic greed. The title echoes the words of an auctioneer about to bring down the hammer on a sale – the implication being that England is being sold off to the highest bidder. On a simple level, the poem criticises urban sprawl and industrial pollution. However, beneath these criticisms lies a more complex social agenda, together with Larkin's personal concerns about his own aging and mortality.

A **post-colonialist** interpretation of this poem might see Larkin as fighting a rearguard action against loss of Empire: England has lost its colonies and now its own backyard is under threat. Stan Smith, in *Inviolable Voice: History and Twentieth-Century Poetry* (Dublin, 1982), gives a **historicist** interpretation of the poem which draws on Marxist critical theory, pointing out just how value-laden this poem is. Larkin the privileged aesthete sees the village boys as 'louts' (4), but accepts them in their place – climbing trees. In stanza 2, the 'bleak high-risers' (11) may refer to blocks of high-rise flats, which might be seen as essential housing to those who cannot afford to live in pretty cottages. On the other hand it may refer to the actual inhabitants of these buildings.

Similarly, in stanza 4 Larkin condemns 'The crowd . . . in the M1 café' for wanting 'More houses, more parking allowed,/ More caravan sites, more pay' (19–23), emphasising the outrageousness of their demands by his use of repetition. On the other hand one could regard these things as legitimate desires. Significantly, Larkin tells us that this 'crowd' is 'young', and that it is their children 'screaming' (16–18) for more, revealing his dislike of children, and perhaps hinting that these people should not be having so many of

QUESTION
From a reading of 'Going, Going', how much do you feel Larkin cared about the environment, as opposed to simply wanting to preserve the England with which he was familiar?

CONTEXT
Larkin's *Collected Poems* gives the date for 'Going, Going' as 25 January 1972. At this time, Britain's miners were on strike, leading to a national crisis, in response to which Edward Heath's Conservative government instituted the three-day working week to conserve energy. The miners won a pay increase and returned to work on 28 February. These events are noticeably absent from this poem.

them. Moreover, at the start of the same stanza he comments on his own age, and since a major theme of the poem is Larkin's own mortality, we might suspect him of resenting these mostly working-class young families.

Stan Smith argues that Larkin, while criticising ordinary people, tries to present himself as ordinary – not privileged – by his use of **colloquial** language, in **stanza** 3 – 'Chuck filth' (16), and especially in stanza 7: 'That before I snuff it, the whole/ Boiling will be bricked in' (38–9). The same could be said of the phrase 'a cast of crooks and tarts' (43), which is presumably a rather cheap and sexist jibe at the government. If Larkin is trying to win our sympathies by this language, he employs a similar trick when he trails off at the end of 'You try to get near the sea/ In summer . . .' (31–2), trying to make us complicit with him by assuming that we would all make the same complaint and can therefore fill in the rest of the sentence. If it is difficult to get near the sea, it is only because of people, like Larkin himself, wanting to go there. We are reminded of his poem 'To the Sea'.

It should also be pointed out that Larkin's England is very much his own idealised and romantic view of what is desirable in it:

> The shadows, the meadows, the lanes,
> The guildhalls, the carved choirs. (37–8)

Others might regard other aspects of the nation's welfare as being more important. Moreover, Larkin's vision excludes the other parts of the United Kingdom – Scotland, Wales and Northern Ireland – not to mention Britain's multicultural society. True, the poem does express environmental concerns, but only rather vaguely (see 27–30).

In the final stanza Larkin questions even the existence of human intention, in the line 'Most things are never meant./ This won't be, most likely' (50–1). The prosaic nature of the language here suggests the matter-of-fact way in which England as he knows it will be eliminated. This idea of events being unintended but inevitable is found again in 'Homage to a Government'.

CHECK THE NET

When *High Windows* was published, approximately 6 per cent of the total UK population was foreign-born. Go to **www.statistics.gov. uk** for immigration statistics and follow the following links: UK Snapshot> Focus on> People & Migration> Foreign-born. See also **www.bbc.co.uk** (search for 'immigration' for a number of relevant pages).

The rhythm of the poem is brisk and fluid, and the rhyme scheme is neat, orderly and unobtrusive, reflecting the casual ease with which Larkin's England is apparently being wiped out. The **enjambment**, especially between stanzas, underlines the idea of an easy slide into an unintended transition from Old England to its modern counterpart.

CHECK THE BOOK

Larkin's idealised view of Old England is in some ways similar to that of another poet whom he admired, and who was a personal friend – Sir John Betjeman. A recent edition of his poems is *The Best of Betjeman* (John Murray, 2006).

GLOSSARY	
4	**louts** uncultured working-class youths
20	**M1** the first motorway in Britain, running northwards from London
24	**Business Page** a page in a newspaper giving business news
	a score twenty
26	**takeover bid** one company's attempt to take over another by making an offer (a bid) to the shareholders of another, usually to buy their shares at higher than the market price
29	**dales** a scenic rural area of Yorkshire
30	**Grey area grants** a witty play on 'Green Area Grants' offered to businesses building on greenfield sites. Larkin's phrase implies turning the 'unspoilt dales' grey with concrete
37	**whole Boiling** a **colloquial** phrase meaning the whole of something
38	**guildhalls** medieval civic buildings
	carved choirs decoratively carved stalls (often medieval) on which the church choir sits

THE CARD-PLAYERS

- The poet describes the scene inside a seventeenth-century Dutch tavern.
- It is a wet and windy night.
- One character goes outside to urinate, then returns.
- The poet comments on the scene.

In this poem Larkin describes the humble scene inside what appears to be a Dutch tavern. There are four characters: Jan van Hogspeuw, Dirk Dogstoerd, Old Prijck and an unnamed drinker. Their very ordinary humanity is expressed through their actions. Jan staggers drunkenly to the door to urinate. Dirk pours himself another drink and lights his pipe. Old Prijck sleeps, while an unnamed man opens mussels and sings, apparently ignored by the others. Outside the night is wild and wet. Inside there is food and drink, warmth and company. Jan 'farts' (12) and spits at the fire, hitting a card – the queen of hearts. In the final line the poet comments ambivalently on the scene.

COMMENTARY

This poem is unusual for Larkin in that it moves beyond his usual sphere of personal experience and modern English life. The poem is reminiscent of paintings by one of the school of Dutch and Flemish painters who sought to find beauty in humble and even morally questionable scenes. It is full of visual details – such as the 'queen of hearts' in the penultimate line (13). The names of the men are humorous parodies of stereotypical Dutch spelling. The four characters described are not in any way heroic or even exceptional. In fact, the names of the three who are named suggest that they are morally degraded and animal-like. 'Hogspeuw' (1) suggests both pigs and drunken vomiting, 'Dogstoerd' (4) canine defecation, 'Old Prijck' (6) exhausted sexuality. All four are probably drunk, as shown by Jan's staggering and Old Prijck's ability to sleep through a gale. Both the other men are drinking, and the unspecific phrase 'some more' (4) suggests a casual familiarity with the drink.

The coarse humanity of these men is emphasised by their bodily functions and by the language used to describe them. Jan urinates into the night, Dirk belches, Old Prijck snores, and the unnamed man's singing is described as croaking – like that of a frog, perhaps because of alcohol and tobacco. There is a hint of censure in the description of Old Prijck's face looking like a skull in the firelight. This detail, as if from a painting, reminds us that despite the inevitability of death these men are frittering away their time in drunken card-playing. However, if the darkness of the night is a **metaphor** for death, then Jan's pissing 'at the dark' (2) could be seen as a sign either of his ignorance of the inevitability of death, or

CONTEXT

Painters such as Pieter Breughel the Younger (1564–1638) and David Teniers the Younger (1610–90) painted tavern scenes like the one depicted in 'The Card-Players'. Tavern card players were a popular subject in their time and continued to be so for many years afterwards. There is a famous painting by Paul Cezanne (1839–1906) called 'Card Players'.

of his nonchalant dismissal of it. Perhaps he is determined to observe the popular saying 'Eat, drink and be merry, for tomorrow we die'.

Larkin's attitude to the scene is ambivalent. The men are coarse, but the scene is not entirely unpleasant and nor does Larkin wholly condemn them. There is plenty of food and drink – there are mussels and the rafters are hung with hams. There is a fire for warmth, and the phrase 'lamplit cave' (12), while hinting at the primitive nature of cavemen, also suggests a cosy shelter from the elements. In addition, the four men seem to be at ease in each other's company. The night outside in a sense presents a threat. The 'century-wide' trees (10) suggest a timelessness that contrasts with the ephemeral nature of the tavern scene, yet their violent clashing as they are blown by the storm is also in contrast to the peaceful scene within. There is also a connection between the outside and inside. The rain is echoed by Jan relieving himself, the wind in the trees by the belching and farting inside. The 'cart-ruts down the deep mud lane' (3) reflect the low moral and social standing of the card-players.

The final line sums up Larkin's mixed-feelings as well as the intense contrast between the elements outside and the shelter within. There is something primeval about the scene, suggested by the simple 'Rain, wind and fire', and the word 'secret' (14) conjures up a cosy security. The men are bestial but they are at peace. Larkin's use of an exclamation mark suggests that, while he finds the scene alien, he is also excited by it.

This is one of two **sonnets** in the collection. It is interesting that Larkin has chosen a poetic form normally associated with more elevated subject matter in which to depict this vulgar scene. It is also of interest that Larkin has chosen a form of the sonnet which is closer to the Italian than the English. The rhyme scheme – ABBA, CDDC, EFEGGE – is basically Italian. However, the rhyming couplet in lines 12–13 is reminiscent of a Shakespearean sonnet, as is the final line, in which 'peace' (14) is a half-rhyme with 'trees' (10). The rhyming couplet of lines 12–13 provides an amusing contrast, rhyming 'farts' and 'hearts' to contrast the profane with the romantic. Jan's action is accidental in that he simply misses the fire,

CHECK THE NET

Go to **www.en.wikipedia.org** for more information on the various forms of the sonnet.

yet it suggests a rejection of romance – by Jan and perhaps by Larkin. This links to the **ironic** description of the unnamed man singing about love in this degraded place. He sings only 'scraps of songs' (9), perhaps because he is drunk, but also perhaps because the songs, like love itself, are only dimly remembered.

The poem is in **iambic pentameter**, as English **sonnets** usually are. However, Larkin varies this to fit his meaning. In fact the first line is one syllable short of the required ten, which causes the line to 'stagger' (1) like Jan.

> **GLOSSARY**
>
> | | |
> |---|---|
> | 5 | **clay** clay pipe |
> | 13 | **gobs** clears his throat and spits |

THE BUILDING

- Larkin describes a hospital, in which patients wait to be summoned for tests or treatment.

- He sees the hospital as offering the only kind of hope, in the face of mortality, that we can expect in the absence of religious belief.

This poem is one of Larkin's most bleak and menacing. It comes in a long line of poems throughout his career in which he tried to come to terms with the stark inevitability of death, such as 'Going' (*The Less Deceived*, 1955) and 'Ambulances' (*The Whitsun Weddings*, 1964). As in 'Friday Night in the Royal Station Hotel', a building is used to create atmosphere. However, 'Friday Night' is all about an empty building and the feelings it stirs, but 'The Building' is also about the inhabitants and how their behaviour reveals their attitude towards death. The poem's menace comes from the enigmatic treatment of its subject: Larkin avoids spelling out that the building is a hospital. He treats it as an atheistic cathedral, the only hope left to us in an increasingly atheistic society.

CONTEXT

Larkin's poem 'Going' describes death in a similarly circumspect way to 'The Building', and with as little hope: 'When it is drawn up over the knees and breast/ It brings no comfort.' However, 'Ambulances' is more closely related to 'The Building'. It describes ambulances using religious **imagery** – they are 'Closed like confessionals' – and its line 'All streets in time are visited' comments on how death comes to all, as does 'Each gets up and goes/ At last' in 'The Building'. The earlier poem also makes a similar contrast between the death-denial of everyday life and the inescapable truth.

COMMENTARY

This poem is in part the fulfilment of an idea Larkin began to explore in another poem, 'How', written in 1970 not long before 'The Building'. In the earlier poem, Larkin writes:

> How high they build hospitals!
> Lighted cliffs, against dawns
> Of days people will die on.

'The Building' splits the image of 'Lighted cliffs' into two – 'lucent comb' (2) and 'clean-sliced cliff' (60), and focuses more closely on the theme of death than the earlier poem does. Larkin begins his account outside the building. It can be seen from afar, and resembles a lit-up honeycomb, perhaps emphasising the busy-ness of its workers and the way in which individuals within it are depersonalised, like bees in a hive. Its height is mentioned again in **stanza** 4 as evidence of its importance. The comparison with 'the handsomest hotel' (1) suggests that what it represents outweighs any material comfort that the commercial world can offer. The comparison comes to mind again in stanza 5, when we see the ever-receding doors and rooms. In the hospital, however, the 'guests' might never leave, and its porters are 'scruffy' (5), having no need to impress the clientele. It is also, notably, a modern building, signifying a modern 'post-Christian' outlook, in contrast with the Victorian streets and church in stanza 6. Hence it is also contrasted in stanza 1 with the hilly streets of terraced ('close-ribbed') Victorian housing which surround it 'like a great sigh out of the last century' (3–4).

The poem balances a sense of unspoken menace with a studied ordinariness. The ambulances that 'keep drawing up' in stanza 1 (5) are not named as such: they are merely not the taxis that we would expect outside a hotel. The pot-plant 'creepers' hanging in the hall combine with the 'frightening smell' (7) to create a sense of unease.

The second stanza describes the apparently everyday details of the place – the 'tea at so much a cup' (8) and the 'half-filled shopping bags' (12), but stanza 4 highlights the oddness of these people being in this place at 'Half-past eleven on a working day' (27). Those who

CHECK THE NET

Larkin based 'The Building' on Hull Royal Infirmary. For information on this hospital, together with an image, go to **www.yecsa.org** and click on Royal Hull NHS Trust.

wait do so 'tamely' (9), like children hoping to appease a feared authority figure. Like the elderly in 'The Old Fools', they have already lost their ability to choose. They simply wait to be fetched away (and not even by a real nurse), as if being chosen by death itself. We see the importance of choice again in the next **stanza**: the people are 'at that vague age that claims/ The end of choice, the last of hope' (20–1).

CHECK THE FILM

Philadelphia (dir. Jonathan Demme, 1993) stars Tom Hanks as a man fired from his job when it is discovered he has AIDS. The latter part of the film is set in hospital, where the character meets death with dignity. *Wit* (dir. Mike Nichols, 2001) stars Emma Thompson as a professor who dies in hospital of cancer, again with considerable dignity.

The passivity of these people is underlined by the word 'confess' (22) at the start of the next stanza, which also hints at the way in which the hospital now takes the place of the cathedral, since there is no longer any comfort to be had in religion. This is signified by the locked church in stanza 6. They are in 'error' (23), as if they have sinned, and the levels to which they climb are 'appointed' (29), as if decreed by God. They are to join 'The unseen congregations' (54) (as in a church service) in stanza 8. Appropriately fearful, they react with nervous displacement activity (stanza 3). Poignantly, their eyes 'Go to each other, guessing' (30), as if they might make contact and share their plight. But when 'Someone's wheeled past, in washed-to-rags ward clothes' (31), this spectre of what they will become silences them. To communicate would risk acknowledging the awful truth of mortality. These people have lived in 'self-protecting ignorance' (48), but this must now come to an end.

From stanza 8 the poem moves towards a conclusion, as Larkin begins to spell out what our own conclusion will be – namely, death. The 'unseen congregations' in 'white rows' (54) are patients in wards, but also the dead in their graves. Finally at the start of stanza 9 we are told that 'All know they are going to die' (57). The hospital, whose cliff-like shape suggests a final abrupt end to human life, represents 'a struggle to transcend/ The thought of dying' (60–1). In other words, by offering a limited hope it keeps not death itself but the *thought* of it at bay. The hope, however, is severely limited. Larkin is sure that we cannot avoid 'The coming dark' (63). The religious offering of 'propitiatory flowers' (64) is ultimately futile.

GLOSSARY

2	**lucent**	shining, light-filled
	comb	honeycomb
39	**lagged**	roughly insulated
42	**hair-dos**	hairstyles, especially cheap ones
43	**separates**	a term used by dry-cleaners for skirts and blouses

POSTERITY

- Larkin describes an imagined academic discussing the fact that he is writing the poet's biography for money when he would rather be doing other things.
- The biographer dismissively describes his subject to a colleague.

This poem relates to 'Sympathy in White Major', as in both poems Larkin contemplates how he will be remembered. The title is **ironically** grand, given how dismissive of him Jake Balokowsky is. Larkin creates the caricatured **persona** of a biographer who is completely cynical about his subject. In so doing, the poet comments on biographers, on himself, and, unexpectedly, on the similarities between him and them.

COMMENTARY

This is a poem which according to Andrew Motion (*Philip Larkin*, Methuen, 1982) has been widely misunderstood. Some critics have seen it simply as a slashing attack on the emptiness of the literary academic world. The insultingly named American academic Balokowsky (*Bal* as in 'Boll', *owsky* as in 'Tchaikovsky') appears at first to be pure caricature. He dresses like a student, in 'jeans and sneakers' (4), he has a romantic desire to be a school teacher in Tel Aviv or 'work on Protest Theater' (13), and he drinks Coke – itself a symbol of the vulgarity of American culture. His language is crassly dismissive: 'old fart' (6), 'stinking dead' (10), 'put this bastard on the skids' (11), 'crummy textbook stuff' (16). Moreover, as an academic he is detached from the real world, 'inside/ His air-conditioned cell at Kennedy' (3).

CHECK THE BOOK

The obvious book to read in connection with 'Posterity' is Andrew Motion's 1993 biography *Philip Larkin: A Writer's Life* (Faber). This is a sensitive and sympathetic account of the poet – quite unlike anything one might expect from the pen of Jake Balokowsky.

Larkin's created **persona** is scathingly convincing. Yet as Larkin himself said after the poem had been published, the poet actually has some sympathy with Balokowsky, and even resembles him in some respects:

> I'm sorry if Jake Balokowsky seemed an unfair portrait. As you see, the idea of the poem was imagining the ironical situation in which one's posthumous reputation was entrusted to somebody as utterly unlike oneself as could be. It was only after the poem had been published that I saw that Jake, wanting to do one thing but having to do something else, was really not so unlike me, and indeed had probably unconsciously been drawn to my work for this reason. (Letter to Richard Murphy quoted in Andrew Motion's *Philip Larkin: A Writer's Life*)

There is an interesting conceit in the idea, in **stanza** 1, that Balokowsky has even this page – the one on which this poem is printed – microfilmed for the purposes of his research, and is therefore able to read how he is described. This is **ironic**, as is Larkin's description of Balokowsky's 'slight impatience with his destiny' (5), the formal tone contrasting with the vulgar one in which Balokowsky expresses what is more than 'slight' impatience.

We see a certain sympathy with Balokowsky in the phrase 'air-conditioned cell' (3). It is comfortable, but it is nonetheless imprisoning, as is his relationship with his wife's parents ('Myra's folks' [8]) and his need to support his children. Larkin, too, would perhaps have preferred to dispense with the need to work for money – as a librarian – and he avoided the commitment of marriage and children, partly at least because he wanted to be free to write. However, the other important reason was that, just as he acknowledges in the voice of Balokowsky, he was 'One of those old-type *natural* fouled-up guys' (18), hedged round with emotional difficulties about relationships with the opposite sex. (Larkin refers to this fact again in 'This Be The Verse'.)

The poem also voices Larkin's ambivalence about his fame. He is characteristically self-deprecating, thinking of his own life as dull – he is 'Not out for kicks or something happening' (17), and he is psychologically damaged. However, the fact that he puts these

CHECK THE BOOK

Larkin's poem 'Toads' (*The Less Deceived*, 1955) also considers his ambivalence towards paid work. In 'Toads Revisited' (*The Whitsun Weddings*, 1964) he seems slightly more reconciled to the necessity of work.

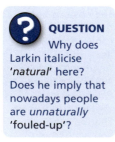

QUESTION
Why does Larkin italicise '*natural*' here? Does he imply that nowadays people are *unnaturally* 'fouled-up'?

words into the mouth of someone like Balokowsky suggests that we should not take his self-criticism at face value.

GLOSSARY

2	**microfilmed** stored in a compact film format for viewing on a reading device (computers were still in their infancy)
3	**Kennedy** an American university named after President John F. Kennedy
4	**sneakers** soft casual shoes, fashionable with the young, named for their quietness
7	**Tel Aviv** a city in Israel; Jake may be Jewish
8	**makes the money sign** draws a dollar symbol in the air with his finger
10	**tenure** a permanent job contract
11	**on the skids** an American slang term short for 'on Skid Row', originally meaning a poor, undesirable part of town. Balokowsky means 'finish him off', but this could be in the sense of completing the biography, or ruining the poet's reputation
12	**semesters** 15–18 week divisions of the US academic year
13	**Protest Theater** politically motivated theatre (note the US spelling)
16	**crummy** a slang term of disparagement (we might say 'rubbishy')
	Freshman Psych the first year of a psychology degree

DUBLINESQUE

- Larkin describes a funeral procession passing along what might be a street in Dublin.

This is an unusually gentle and simply beautiful poem for Larkin, with no trace of bitterness or **irony**. Like many of the poems in this collection, it raises the theme of death, but here the death brings a sense of community, as it does in 'The Explosion' (but notably not in 'The Building'). This sense of community, even of celebration, reflects the Irish tradition of the 'wake'. The mourners are brought

CHECK THE BOOK

D. H. Lawrence's poem *'Giorno dei Morti'* ('Day of the Dead') is also about a funeral procession, though in Italy, and has something of the same atmosphere as Larkin's 'Dublinesque'.

together as friends as they pay tribute to the deceased. The poem commemorates the passing of a loved one, quietly and with dignity.

COMMENTARY

This is another poem of intriguing paradoxes. The 'light is pewter' (2), and therefore dark, like the light in 'Friday Night in the Royal Station Hotel'. A funeral procession is described, yet the mood is gently sad rather than grim. The 'troop of streetwalkers' (9), generally assumed by critics to be prostitutes rather than just pedestrians, are quite gaily, even theatrically, dressed, and the word 'troop' is reminiscent of the circus. There is 'an air of great friendliness' (13), rather than simply of grief; some of the mourners 'caper' (16) while 'Someone claps time' (18), suggesting a light-hearted celebration rather than a sombre occasion. There is 'great sadness' (19), yet there is also singing which evokes 'All love, all beauty' (24).

CHECK THE BOOK

A writer whom Larkin read, at least in his youth, and who is closely associated with Dublin, is James Joyce (1882–1941). Both his book of short stories, *The Dubliners* (1914), and his major work, the novel *Ulysses* (1922), are set in Dublin.

The use of the present tense has the effect of making the account stand outside of time. It also fits with Larkin's description of the scene coming to him in a dream ('I just woke up and described it,' Andrew Motion, *Philip Larkin: A Writer's Life*). The use of the passive sentence form in 'A voice is heard singing' (21) helps to make the poem dreamlike, as it detaches us a little, making the narrator less visible than if he had written 'I hear a voice singing'.

The predominantly **dactylic** rhythm (stressed, unstressed, unstressed) fits a funeral procession more than, say, an **iambic** one would (as in 'This Be The Verse'). It seems to move in step, at a walking pace. The dim, misty light also fits a funeral. The **metre** is fairly regular, though the lack of rhyme suggests the relative informality of the event. **Stanza** 1 even imitates the winding of the procession. The sentence itself processes: we have to wait until the last line to discover its subject – a funeral. The **alliterative** 'race-guides and rosaries' (5) is lyrical, at the same time juxtaposing betting shops and Catholicism. The phrase 'wend away' (20) in stanza 4 is similarly lyrical, and suggests the slowly snaking movement of the passing procession.

Assuming that the 'streetwalkers' (9) are prostitutes, Larkin's attitude towards them is interesting. He so often demonstrates ambivalent attitudes towards sex, yet these women, following the coffin of someone who was presumably also a prostitute, are described with respect and sensitivity. Their hats and sleeves are showy, but their dresses are demurely ankle-length. They show a sense of community and honour, and when they dance it is 'skilfully' (17). Moreover, the singing voice appears to belong to someone of refined sensibilities.

The 'Kitty, or Katy' (22) is an interesting detail. It could be that Larkin simply cannot be sure what he heard in his dream, but the poetic effect is to make the individual identity of the deceased vague, and therefore less important than the love and beauty for which she stands.

> **CONTEXT**
>
> The name Kitty in 'Dublinesque' may be that of Larkin's older sister Catherine, known as Kitty – although she outlived him.

GLOSSARY

1	**stucco** a cement mixture used to cover an unattractive building material
2	**pewter** a metal alloy consisting mostly of tin, but with smaller amounts of copper and lead
5	**rosaries** sets of Catholic prayer beads
9	**Leg-of-mutton sleeves** long sleeves, puffed out on the upper arm and more close-fitting lower down

---

HOMAGE TO A GOVERNMENT

- Larkin comments ironically on the government's intention to bring home troops from abroad.
- He explains that this is all to save money.

This poem is an **ironic** political comment on the decision made by Harold Wilson's Labour Government to withdraw British troops from east of Suez. The poem appears to be both patriotic and anti-materialist, though it is difficult to say which element is the stronger. It comments on posterity, in a different way from the poem of that name, suggesting that leaving the troops abroad would in some way give 'Our children' (17) a better inheritance than bringing them home.

CONTEXT

'Homage to a Government' was originally called 'Homage to a Prime Minister'. Harold Wilson's decision to withdraw all British troops from east of Suez was made in the wake of the final withdrawal in 1968 of troops from the former British colony of Aden in the Persian Gulf, in the face of uncontrollable violence. Larkin told an interviewer: 'I don't mind troops being brought home if we'd decided this was the best thing all round, but to bring them home simply because we couldn't afford to keep them there seemed a dreadful humiliation.' (*Required Writing*, Faber, 1983).

COMMENTARY

This is a poem of opinions and values. The title is bitterly **ironic**: Larkin does not actually regard the Wilson government as being worthy of 'homage', which implies honour. Rather, he considers that to bring the soldiers home merely for economic reasons is dishonourable. However, Larkin was not an astute political analyst, and, whether or not he was right to disagree with the Prime Minister's decision, he puts forward no convincing arguments against bringing the troops home. Rather, he concentrates on making the arguments in favour sound weak and dishonourable.

Larkin perhaps dislikes the idea of living in an impoverished Britain, though one could argue that it is more a question of economic priorities than real hardship. The repeated variants on 'and it is all right' (2, 6, 10) are deliberately weak and drab in their wording, suggesting something similar in the character of those who believe in them. There is also an implied weakness in those who simply want the money 'Instead of working' (6) and who have allowed the political decision to be made without really knowing 'who wanted it to happen' (7). It appears to be a decision by default, endorsed by inertia: 'now it's been decided nobody minds' (8). Even the location of the places, 'a long way off' (9), is bland, as if echoing the feeble platitudes of those who have let this happen. Moreover, these faceless commentators are presented as happy to accept the hearsay opinion that 'The soldiers there only made trouble happen' (11). As in 'The Old Fools' and 'The Building', Larkin presents the loss or giving up of real choice as a step towards death.

The final **stanza** is rhythmically stronger, as the poet moves from **satirising** a view to presenting his own. The image of statues, many of which commemorate England's past heroes, standing in 'Tree-muffled' squares (16) – 'muffled' perhaps suggesting that they have been silenced – is an evocative one, but one might question whether Larkin is manipulating the reader's feelings here. The message is persuasively anti-materialistic, but one wonders just what 'Our children' (17) would be left had the money still been spent on maintaining an army abroad.

One feature of the poem is its deliberately flat monotone and almost image-free language, reflecting the drabness to which Larkin feels materialism has brought us. This is increased by the repetition of 'it is all right', but also of the words at the ends of lines (1 and 5, 2 and 6, 3 and 4).

THIS BE THE VERSE

- Larkin comments on how one generation passes its psychological problems on to the next.
- He concludes that the solution is to die (or leave home) as soon as possible and not have any children.

Though not entirely representative of Larkin, this poem has become one of his best known, because of its shockingly **colloquial** and transparent language, its vigorous, bouncy rhythm and simple rhyme scheme, and its straightforward message. It reflects Larkin's personal difficulties with relationships, though it does at least acknowledge them openly and without apology. However, one should guard against oversimplifying the poem by assuming that Larkin is simply stating his own views rather than adopting a **persona**. It is also worth noting that, despite the light tone, the poem deals with weighty matters.

COMMENTARY

This is a poem of popular post-Freudianism. At the time when it was written, psychoanalysis was becoming well-known, and the general public were therefore becoming familiar with the idea that everyone is to some extent psychologically damaged by their parenting. It seems to reflect Larkin's own problems in relationships, blaming them by implication on his parents. It is in a sense a partner to 'Annus Mirabilis', in which the emphasis is on sexual repression rather than on parents. Larkin wrote on more than one occasion about the misery of his parents' marriage. His father was remote, and insisted that his wife Eva should confine herself to home-making, and yet despised her for it. His mother was unfulfilled, and both parents bickered. Larkin claimed that this

> **CONTEXT**
>
> Many modern writers have been influenced by the theories of Sigmund Freud (1856–1939). In particular he held that repressed sexual impulses were responsible for much human behaviour, and that unconscious sexuality often revealed itself symbolically in dreams.

CHECK THE BOOK

A number of biblical passages assert that 'the sins of the fathers shall be visited upon their sons': Exodus 20:5; Numbers 14:18; Deuteronomy 5:9; Jeremiah 32:17. Larkin parodies this by replacing God with inept parents. The jokey nature of this **allusion** is perhaps assured by a comment Larkin made in the *London Magazine* (November, 1964): 'to me . . . the whole of classical and biblical mythology means very little.'

CONTEXT

The first line of **stanza** 3 is reminiscent of Thomas Hardy (1840–1928), a poet who influenced Larkin. Hardy, for example, wrote of 'the monotonous moils of strained, hard-run humanity', and generally saw human life as one of suffering.

deterred him from ever getting married himself. He also avowedly disliked children, so it is unsurprising that in this poem he counsels against having them. On the other hand, his reason is presumably to save them from his own fate.

The evocative phrase 'fools in old-style hats and coats' (6) suggests family photos – a modern record of preceding generations – while the **alliterative** 'soppy-stern' (7) succinctly sums up the older generation's inconsistent and psychologically damaging parenting.

The poem's title, though recalling the Old Testament, is taken from a poem by Robert Louis Stevenson, which was engraved on Stevenson's gravestone:

> . . . This be the verse you grave for me:
> *Here he lies where he longed to be;*
> *Home is the sailor, home from sea,*
> *And the hunter home from the hill.*

The speaker of this poem dictates his own epitaph, and Larkin's poem can therefore be seen as a kind of epitaph for himself, or at least a requiem. The phrase 'Man hands on misery to man' (9) also alludes to the Bible, where it is written that 'the sins of the fathers shall be visited upon their sons', for several generations to come.

The structure of the poem is simple but effective, the first **stanza** stating the problem, the second explaining its origins, and the third revealing both the wider implications and the solution. In addition each stanza ends with a twist. In the first, it is the **ironic** 'treat' of being given one's own special faults; in the second it is the abrupt switch from ineptitude to murder, and in the third it is the contrast between the rather weighty first two lines, including the arresting image of the 'coastal shelf' (10), and the glib advice of the last two lines.

GLOSSARY

10	**coastal shelf** a geological term for an extension of a land mass for some distance beneath a shallow sea before dropping off into deeper water. Such a shelf may 'deepen' in time as more sediment is deposited

HOW DISTANT

- Larkin considers the freedom and opportunities of youth, in the context of emigration.

This is a wonderfully wistful poem about youth, opportunity, and the freedom to make big, sweeping choices about one's life. This freedom is 'distant' in that it happened in the past – 'assisted passage' was a scheme giving financial assistance to people wishing to emigrate to Australia. However, it is also distant in that this freedom is remote from the circumstances of the poet – an aging librarian. Perhaps, too, it is distant in that no one is ever really as free as the poem suggests. Larkin, then, could be offering a consciously idealised, though wistful, view of the freedom of 'inventing' (19) one's life.

CONTEXT
After the Second World War, Australia encouraged immigration by offering 'assisted passage'. Would-be immigrants, known as 'Ten Pound Poms', only had to pay £10 towards their fare. Between 1945 and 1972, over a million British migrants took advantage of this offer.

COMMENTARY

This poem offers a contrast to 'This Be The Verse'. In the better-known poem, opportunity is severely limited by the psychological damage done in childhood; in 'How Distant', the young have the world before them. All is bright and optimistic, the stuff of dreams: the 'green shore past the salt-white cordage' (3), the sweet music of melodeons, the fantasies conjured by the glimpse of a girl doing her laundry. Being young is 'Like new store clothes' (17) as opposed to hand-me-downs. Their 'huge decisions' (18) invent their lives. Life presents chance opportunities, as if by magic: 'random windows conjuring a street' (20).

The poem swings between the young men leaving their villages and those already on the ship bound for Australia. Their keenness to get away is reflected in the sharp-edged **alliteration** of 'Cattlemen, or carpenters, or keen' (5). They may have a trade to pursue in the new country or they may just want to escape pressure to marry ('married villages', [7]) or even escape their wives – which would explain their leaving at night. Alternatively, 'married villages' could mean those where most people are already married, and where it is difficult to find a wife. This is a case of Larkin's compactness of expression making his intention unclear.

QUESTION
Which of the possible meanings for 'married villages' do you find most convincing?

There is a sense of dynamic movement, partly in the prospect of travel itself, and partly in the image of the shore 'Rising and falling' (4) from the perspective of the sea, and that of the 'fraying cliffs of water' (9). The stars are perhaps 'differently-swung' (11) because they are constellations visible in the Southern Hemisphere, or simply because of the movement of the ship. The sight of a girl doing her laundry is sexually exciting, and all the more so because it is only glimpsed, like the prospects of Australia itself. The word 'Ramifies' (14), literally means 'develops', but it also has connotations of raw male sexuality.

The last sentence of the poem comments on the concrete images presented up to this point, in a series of more abstract images in which Larkin attempts to convey what 'being young' (15) is. The key image, as in 'High Windows' is of the 'windows conjuring a street' (20) in the final line. They are, in the more popular phrase, 'windows of opportunity', and the street to which they lead is a symbol of the unknown future.

> **? QUESTION**
> The phrase 'Assumption of the startled century' suggests a confident ability to seize time rather than being subject to it. Do you think it has a more precise meaning?

GLOSSARY

3	**cordage** rope strung along the edge of a ship's deck to prevent people from falling overboard
8	**melodeons** a type of button accordion popular at sea because they are easy to transport and store
13	**steerage** part of a ship providing cheap accommodation

SAD STEPS

- Larkin comments self-mockingly on a moonlit sky.
- He is reminded of his youth.

In this unusual poem, Larkin draws our attention to the visual effect of a moonlit sky, only to undermine his own lyricism by self-parody. The moon brings romantic images to mind, but he mocks these, even as they arise in his imagination. He replaces them with a harsher picture of youth which the moon also suggests to him.

The 'Sad Steps' of the title are those of the poet, of the passing of time, and of the moon's climbing in the sky.

COMMENTARY

Like one or two other poems in *High Windows*, this begins with **colloquial** profanity, which is soon replaced by something compellingly beautiful, and then by a profound idea. The central symbol of the poem is the moon, so in a sense this is an **ode** celebrating a single subject and exploring the ideas it generates.

Larkin admits to being 'startled' (2) by the night sky. The scene from the window is unusual, in that the tame suburban gardens are seen at night, 'wedge-shadowed' (4), and beneath a wild sky. Perhaps this contrast between the sublime and the mundane is what Larkin finds ridiculous. The way the moon 'dashes' (7), as in a hurry, is perhaps slightly comical too, though the image of the clouds blowing 'Loosely as cannon-smoke' (8) is beautiful rather than comic, as is the parenthesised note on the way the light sharpens the roofs below. In **stanza** 3, Larkin suddenly ridicules the moon, or rather his own associations with it. Its 'preposterous' separateness (10) summons absurd parodies of romantic poetry. It is a 'Lozenge of love' (round like a lozenge, but then a lozenge is a cough sweet!), and a 'Medallion of art' (11). It awakens 'wolves of memory' (12), perhaps savagely hunting down memories he would rather not revisit. The last of these parodies is a made-up word – 'Immensements' (12), which suggests poetic attempts at self-aggrandising. It is also a pun: *mensis* is the Latin for 'month', a period of time based on the lunar cycle. The sudden collapse of these exclamations is brought by the one word 'No' (12), emphasised by its positioning at the end of the stanza.

The final two stanzas embody a more sober view. Larkin is struck simply by the 'hardness and the brightness' of the moon (14), and by its singularity. He **personifies** it as possessing a 'wide stare' (15). This chills him ('One shivers slightly' [13]), reminding him of youth. He may also be literally chilled, as a full moon high in the sky at 'Four o'clock' (4) indicates that this is a winter night. In addition, the fullness of the moon perhaps **symbolises** the potential of youth, which wanes like the moon as one ages. Larkin's memory of youth is ambivalent – there is strength, as in 'How Distant', but

> **CONTEXT**
>
> Shakespeare occasionally uses **imagery** related to clothing, as in 'Like new store clothes'. For example, in *Macbeth*, Macbeth himself says: 'I have bought/ Golden opinions from all sorts of people/ Which would be worn now in their newest gloss' (Act I, scene 7).

CHECK THE NET

The moon has been the subject of many poems, especially by Romantic poets. William Wordsworth (1770–1850) wrote several, including one which Larkin may have had in mind: 'With How Sad Steps, O Moon, Thou Climb'st The Sky'. Read this poem at **www. bartleby.com**

there is also pain. However, one suspects that the pain is as much that of the elderly Larkin regretting his lost youth, as it is of actual youth. Nonetheless, as in other poems (such as 'High Windows'), he moves in the final two lines to an idea transcending the limitations of the personal: he consoles himself with the thought that although his own youth cannot return, at least youth itself continues 'for others undiminished somewhere' (18).

The **metre** is relatively slow and considered, as befits a contemplative poem, and the subtle and regular rhyme scheme holds the ideas of the poem together unobtrusively. The words which rhyme are thrown into a slightly closer relationship with each other than if they had not rhymed. Thus the vulgarity of the first line fits with the 'something laughable' of the sixth, with which it rhymes.

SOLAR

- The poet contemplates the enduring generosity of the sun.

This surprising poem about the sun is unique in the collection as an unabashed paean of praise to nature. It is also a kind of **Symbolist ode**, focusing on the symbolic value of material objects and the musical properties of language. Appropriately, it faces 'Sad Steps', whose subject is the moon, yet its tone is quite different. It is in **free verse**, without rhyme or any obvious **metre**, which is also unusual for Larkin. It is also, in one sense, simple in its close focus on a single inanimate object.

COMMENTARY

There are no human characters in this poem, until the sun's constancy is compared with the changeability of humanity in the final **stanza**. Instead, we have a series of images with which the sun is compared: a lion and a flower (perhaps a dandelion or a sunflower) in stanzas 1 and 2, and a gold coin and a hand in stanza 3. The poem is a tribute to the sun's constant, unrewarded, self-sufficient pouring out of heat. The sky in which it spills is 'unfurnished' (3), like an empty room. The sun seems to **symbolise**

CONTEXT

The sun has been associated with lions, for example in its 'rulership' of the astrological sign of Leo, for at least 3,000 years.

the sole, impersonal, energy at the heart of the universe. Its self-sufficiency is in contrast to recurring human needs (see stanza 3), especially the need for company.

There is balance in the poem between movement and stillness, change and constancy. The sun's 'lion face' is 'Spilling' yet 'still' (1–4); it pours out energy, 'Continuously exploding' (12) but never needs to be replenished. Often Larkin associates money with drab materialism, as in 'How Distant' and 'Money', yet here, as gold coin, it seems to represent pure energy. The importance of 'Gold' (14) is highlighted by its appearing on its own line. The sun itself has no needs, and the 'Lonely horizontals' (16) among which it exists are lonely only to the human observer. Our needs are said to be like angels, perhaps those which climb 'Jacob's ladders' in cathedral architecture. This hints at the angelic aspect of human character, but it also highlights our neediness. The sun, by contrast, simply gives out warmth and light. Larkin's 'Unclosing like a hand' (20) is a wonderful image for this cosmic generosity.

Andrew Motion writes of this poem: 'Larkin adopts the dislocations, illogicalities and imaginative excitement of symbolism to redeem himself from distressing daily circumstances' ('Philip Larkin and Symbolism' in, Stephen Regan [ed.], *Philip Larkin: Contemporary Critical Essays*, Palgrave Macmillan, 1997). There is also a great calmness in the short, slow-moving lines, which seems to raise them above this mundane level.

ANNUS MIRABILIS

- Larkin comments wryly on the social history of sex.
- He thinks about his having missed out on the 'free love' of the 1960s.

Like 'This Be The Verse', this poem is well known because of its entertainingly glib opening and apparently simple message. It can easily be read as Larkin complaining about his having missed out on sex, but we know that this was at least not entirely the case (even if he did as an undergraduate), so we should guard against

CONTEXT

In the Bible, after Jacob had tricked his brother Esau out of his birthright and obtained his father's blessing, he had a vision of angels ascending and descending a ladder that stretched from earth to heaven. God stood at the top of the ladder. Images or models of such ladders are found in some churches and cathedrals.

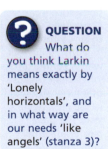

QUESTION
What do you think Larkin means exactly by 'Lonely horizontals', and in what way are our needs 'like angels' (stanza 3)?

taking this as uncomplicated confessional verse (see **Background: Philip Larkin's life and work**). However, there is a strong element of **ironic** social comment. If Larkin is not telling us about himself, he is certainly telling us about the times in which he lived.

COMMENTARY

This poem partners 'This Be The Verse', but the emphasis here is on sex. Its opening is arresting because it is ridiculous to think that something as old as sexual intercourse actually started in 1963 – as if one could pinpoint the year. It actually refers to the 'sexual liberation' of the 1960s, and especially to the introduction of the contraceptive pill into Britain in 1963, but Larkin avoids spelling this out. The title of the poem, meaning 'Miracle Year', adds to the humour. The rather plaintive 'Which was rather late for me' (3) is also entertaining, because we imagine the poet, or an imagined **persona**, regretting in this unassuming and understated way that he has missed out on a major human experience. The placing of this date between two events associated with sex helps to make the unjustifiable statement more credible.

The poem can be compared with 'High Windows', which also comments satirically on the sexual liberation of the 1960s. There, Larkin suggests that the sexual liberation is not the paradise that the older generation expected, and in 'Annus Mirabilis' the exaggeratedly positive comment on the new era cannot possibly be taken at face value: 'A brilliant breaking of the bank,/ A quite unlosable game' (14–15). No game is unlosable and the idea that every life is guaranteed to be successful is clearly ridiculous. The sudden uniformity of feeling ('Everyone felt the same' [12]) is also unbelievable – and even if it were believable, it would still be undesirable. Nor can we take literally the conclusion that 'life was never better' (16). Larkin never describes life as getting better, except ironically. And more often, as in 'Going, Going', it gets worse. We can therefore fairly safely assume that he is being ironic here, even if there is an element of actual envy of the young present as well.

'Annus Mirabilis' is also similar to other poems in the collection in its attitude towards marriage. In 'High Windows' it is represented as 'Bonds and gestures pushed to one side' (6) by the new era; in

CHECK THE BOOK

D. H. Lawrence published *Lady Chatterley's Lover* privately in Florence in 1928. An expurgated version was published in London in 1932. Constance Chatterley is married to Sir Clifford, a wealthy landowner who is confined to a wheelchair because of injuries sustained in the First World War. She has a passionate affair with the gamekeeper, Oliver Mellors, the son of a miner. When Penguin Books printed a full version in 1960, they were prosecuted under the Obscene Publications Act (1959) but were acquitted. Lawrence himself had died in 1930.

'Annus Mirabilis' it is 'A sort of bargaining,/ A wrangle for a ring' (7–8). Similarly, in 'How Distant', the young men are keen to get away from 'married villages' (7). However, one cannot simply regard Larkin as anti-marriage either, because the 'free love' alternative is not presented as a real improvement. Larkin's underlying view that 'Man hands on misery to man' ('This Be The Verse' [9]) is ever present. One wonders if Larkin even believes that the 'shame that started at sixteen/ And spread to everything' (9–10) (like the 'sweating in the dark' of 'High Windows', [12]) has completely ended in the new era.

The poem, unusually, is in five-line **stanzas**. The lively, basically **iambic** rhythm trips along very easily, aided by a regular rhyme scheme, quite like the lyrics of a song. This reinforces the meaning of the poem – nothing is really that easy. The rhythm is particularly bouncy in stanza 3, which is all about the new era, until we reach the stanza's last line – 'A quite unlosable game' (15), where an extra syllable adds to the idea of life overflowing after the 'brilliant breaking of the bank' (14). It also forces us to pause before the final stanza.

This last stanza is interesting for the way in which it revisits the first, repeating lines 2, 4 and 5 word for word and only slightly altering line 2. The effect is somehow mournful, perhaps because it suggests that this short period of time was a hey-day from which everything since has declined. There is also a possible parody of Conservative Prime Minister Harold Macmillan's line in a speech to the British people in 1957, 'You've never had it so good'. The line was often quoted ironically, and sometimes still is.

CHECK THE NET

To read the lyrics of the Beatles' first album, *Please, Please Me*, go to:
www.iamthebeatles.com
and search for 'please please me'.

GLOSSARY

4	*Chatterley* **ban** refers to *Lady Chatterley's Lover*, by D. H. Lawrence, banned in Britain until 1960 because of its relatively explicit descriptions of sex (between a working-class man and an upper-class woman) and its use of four-letter words
5	**Beatles' first LP** (Long-Playing record); *Please, Please Me* (named after its title track) was released in March 1963
14	**breaking of the bank** two meanings: the bursting of a dam, and when a gambler wins more money than the gambling house can pay out

CONTEXT

At the time
'Money' was
written (1973),
Britain was
relatively affluent.
At the same time
popular culture
questioned the
value of money.
For example, in
the same year, the
band Pink Floyd
released the album
*Dark Side of the
Moon*, which
included 'Money',
a song satirising
materialism.

MONEY

- The speaker reflects on his failure to make use of what money he has to buy material goods or to pay for sex.
- He considers the role of money in human life.

This is an anti-materialist poem. Larkin, or the speaker, comments on the fact that he has money but does not spend it – as if he cannot quite work out what it is for. He assumes a rather naïve, unworldly ignorance, but still expresses some views on money. You may as well spend it young, since if you wait till you retire you will no longer be young enough to enjoy it. Moreover, money is ultimately useless as you can't take it with you beyond the grave: the 'shave' (12) in **stanza** 3 is presumably that given to a corpse by the undertaker. The final stanza produces one of those transcendent images that one finds in several poems in *High Windows*, as the speaker compares money to a provincial town. However, whereas in the poem 'High Windows' the vision is uplifting, here it is almost the opposite – 'intensely sad' (16).

COMMENTARY

As ever, one should be wary of assuming that the speaker in the poem is simply Larkin talking about himself and his own views. However, as the head librarian of Hull University, Larkin earned a reasonable salary, yet he had no wife or children to support, did not go in for foreign travel, and was not known for a champagne lifestyle. Therefore, he may well have looked at his quarterly bank statements and wondered if he ought to be spending more. Andrew Motion, in *Philip Larkin: A Writer's Life*, assumes that Larkin is talking about himself.

At one level, the poem comments on the world largely being driven by money. That this is a bad thing, and that money is unsatisfying, is suggested in stanza 1 by the description of the people who spend it. The fact that they have a 'second house and car and wife' (7), suggests that Larkin is thinking of men, and that these men not only have material goods, but have probably divorced and remarried.

In stanza 3, Larkin loosely compares money with life, and concludes that one should make the most of youth, since it can't be postponed till retirement, and similarly that one should spend one's money. This is slightly at odds, however, with the **ironically** casual tone of stanza 1, particularly the idea that one might buy sex.

The arrestingly beautiful and mournful final stanza revisits the image of windows found in 'High Windows' and several other poems in this collection – this time 'long french windows' (14) rather than high ones. Money sings like a siren song, offering false promise – like the promise of youth in 'High Windows'. It offers hope and happiness, but in reality, little happiness is possible in a world represented by a provincial town, with its slums, its canal (a reference to nineteenth-century industry) and its 'ornate' but 'mad' churches (15). As in 'The Old Fools', the evening sun somehow makes the scene even sadder.

However, it is also important that the poet, or his **persona**, is looking down on this scene 'From long french windows' (14). Whatever the world offers, he is cut off from it. In 'High Windows' a transcendent vision is possible because the material world is invisible because the windows are high, revealing only the blue sky. Here, the drabness of the real world is all too visible. Even if he wrote 'a few cheques' (4) it would make little difference to his life.

> **CONTEXT**
>
> In Greek mythology, the Sirens were enchantresses who lured men to their deaths by their beautiful singing. In Homer's *Odyssey*, Odysseus has himself strapped to the mast of his ship so that he can hear the Sirens' song without being tempted to join them. His men have to stop their ears with beeswax.

> **GLOSSARY**
>
> 11 **screw** slang term for money – derived either from the idea that it has to be forced out of people using thumb screws or from it being something you screw up in your pocket

CUT GRASS

- Larkin comments on grass mown in summer.

In this short, beautiful and perfectly formed poem, Larkin describes cut grass, personifying it, perhaps as a symbol of the frailty and brevity of human life. The fact that the grass is cut in

June, at a time when the natural world is blooming, makes the description more poignant.

COMMENTARY

This is one of Larkin's **symbolist** poems. Whereas a poet like Ted Hughes might explore the essential energy of the grass, Larkin is only really concerned with it as a symbol for something delicately transitory. Its life is brief, its death 'Long, long' (4), like human death as pictured in 'The Old Fools'.

There is, all the same, a real sense of the natural world. The breath that the 'Mown stalks exhale' (3) suggests the delicate fragrance of newly mown grass. We see a charming picture of 'young-leafed June' (6), which hints at youth as well as life in a more general sense. In the long sentence from line 3 of **stanza** 1 to the end of the poem, Larkin builds up a picture of rural England in early summer, a time of hope. At the same time, the blossom in the hedges is like snow, suggesting winter to come, or old age. The lilac blossom is heavy enough to bow the branches. 'Lost lanes' (10) suggest a rural world into which one might escape from a harsher reality. 'Queen Anne's lace' (10), whilst being an actual plant, also suggests English history of the sort that Larkin regrets passing in 'Going, Going'. There is also a sense of purity: all the flowers mentioned are white.

In the final stanza we move upwards, cinematically, from the idealised rural lanes to the sky overhead. Here, the cloud, itself a nebulous symbol standing for something unobtainable and indefinable, moves at the unhurried 'summer's pace' (12) of old England. Larkin's use of 'high-builded' (11) is striking, not least because it is ungrammatical, but also because it makes us picture the cloud being built up in layers (perhaps like English history), in a way that a more conventional and grammatically correct phrase would not. It may well allude to William Blake's poem 'Jerusalem', which announces the intention to build Jerusalem 'In England's green and pleasant land'. Blake's poem also includes the following stanza:

> And did the Countenance Divine
> Shine forth upon our clouded hills?
> And was Jerusalem builded here
> Among these dark Satanic Mills?

CHECK THE NET

To read about Queen Anne's lace and see images of it, visit www.carrotmuseum. co.uk and search for 'queen anne's lace' to find the plant.

This uses the word 'builded', closely linked to clouds. Blake's pastoral view of England also fits well with Larkin's picture of lost and leafy lanes.

The three-stanza structure of 'Cut Grass' is satisfying in that, loosely speaking, stanza 1 introduces the subject, stanza 2 paints the surrounding scene, and stanza 3 takes us to a kind of conclusion. The rhyme scheme is simple but strict, and perfectly balanced. To a certain extent it is pleasing in itself, but it also serves to draw rhyming words into closer relationship; for example, 'frail' and 'exhale' (1 and 3), already connected in sense, and 'breath' and 'death' (2 and 4), juxtaposed as near-opposites.

CONTEXT

William Blake (1757–1827) was a visionary early Romantic poet whose poems often include a pastoral element. His poem 'Jerusalem' is often sung as a hymn, to music composed by Parry in 1916.

GLOSSARY	
7	**chestnut** popularly known as 'conker trees', these spreading trees usually have white blossom (though sometimes pink), known as candles
9	**lilac** a small tree which can have mauve (lilac), pink or white flowers. It can be found in lanes, but is more likely to be found in gardens, as it is not native to Britain
10	**Queen Anne's lace** wild carrot, a plant growing wild in the verges of English country lanes. It has clusters of small white flowers which resemble lace. Queen Anne reigned from 1702 to 1714. Lace was popular during her reign

THE EXPLOSION

- Miners talk and smoke on their way to work in the pit.
- One man chases rabbits and returns with a nest of lark's eggs.
- A tremor signals an explosion in the pit.
- The men's wives see the dead men in an apparition.

In **stanza** 1 we see shadows pointing ominously towards the pithead, while the slagheap appears to sleep. Into this scene come several men on their way to work in the mine. They seem strong and vigorous in a masculine way, imposing themselves on the silence. One of the men chases rabbits, loses them and returns with a nest of lark's eggs to

CONTEXT

Larkin claimed that 'The Explosion' is based on 'a song about a mine disaster, a ballad, a sort of folk-song. I thought it very moving . . . It made me want to write the same thing, a mine disaster with a vision of immortality at the end'. However, it has also been reported that he wrote the poem after watching a television documentary on the mining industry which was screened at Christmas in 1969.

show his workmates before putting the nest back in the grass. **Stanza** 4 gives us a sense of community and male camaraderie, and we see the men passing through the gates to the mine.

There is an implied passing of time before an earth tremor announces the explosion that has occurred in the pit (stanza 5). Stanza 6 quotes a biblical passage about life after death and the promise of seeing our loved ones in heaven. The last three stanzas describe the doomed men appearing to their wives at the moment of their death, including the man who found the nest of lark's eggs, still carrying them unbroken.

COMMENTARY

This sombre yet mystical poem comes, appropriately, at the end of the collection. It is relatively unusual for Larkin, because it describes what is probably a real-life event which had nothing to do with him personally, set in a world of working-class male camaraderie which to Larkin, as a librarian, was unfamiliar territory. It also contains nothing of Larkin's often sardonic humour. Rather, it is a moving, respectful and mystical poem that depicts a tragedy and even looks towards a possible afterlife.

This is a strongly **narrative** poem. It begins by setting the scene in stanza 1. We are told immediately what the subject of the poem is to be: an explosion in a coalmine. Even before the men appear on the lane, shadows point ominously towards the pithead. The sunshine belies the tragedy that is about to occur and the slagheap, **personified** as sleeping, suggests the men's misplaced sense of security. There is something cinematic about the appearance of the men in stanza 2, as if the camera is poised on the lane, and we see and hear them as they gradually come into view. Their vigorous masculinity is suggested by their pitboots, their conversation casually laced with swearwords, their pipes, and the way they force their way physically into the silence of the morning 'shouldering' it off (6). However, their coughing hints at one of the dangers of working in a mine – the effects of coal dust on the lungs – foreshadowing the disaster to come.

One of the men behaves in a surprisingly boyish and playful way, chasing rabbits and returning with a nest of lark's eggs. There is a touching innocence in the way he shows the nest to his workmates and then returns it to the grass, presumably unharmed. Stanza 4 draws back from the particular instance to a more general description of the men passing which evokes male camaraderie and a community in which the men are either related to each other or are familiar with each other. They laugh together in a relaxed way, and use each other's nicknames. However, there is again a sense of something ominous, or at least prescient, in the mention of the tall gates through which they pass to the mine.

There is an implied passing of time before the start of stanza 5. At noon, an appropriately significant moment, there comes an earth tremor. There is a certain dramatic irony in the fact that the cows stop chewing only for a second. The surface world continues as if nothing has happened, but the sun seems to behave portentously. It is 'dimmed', 'scarfed' (15) – bandaged – in a possible allusion to a line in Shakespeare's *Macbeth*: 'Scarf up the pitiful eye of tender day' (Act III, scene 2).

Stanza 6 presents a sudden jump. It gives a paraphrase of 1 Corinthians 13:12, offering the Christian consolation that the dead are 'not lost, but gone before', that they are sitting comfortably in heaven, and that their loved ones will one day see them again – '*face to face*' (18). These lines were perhaps spoken prior to the explosion in the chapels attended by the men, seeming in retrospect to predict it. This stanza prepares us for stanza 7, which describes a phenomenon known as the *doppelganger*, whereby a ghostly form of a dying person is said to appear to the living. The men appear to their wives in an apparently mystical way. Moreover in death, they seem to be ennobled, 'larger than in life', like gold on a coin (22–3). In stanza 1 the direction of the shadows shows that the men are walking with the sun behind them, from east to west, and now they appear still walking out of the sun, haloed by its light. The final line of the poem is particularly moving as it shows the man who found the lark's nest, still holding it, a symbol of life to come, or of the human spirit. The soaring lark also forms a contrast to the dark days spent by the men underground.

CONTEXT

The 'tall gates' in stanza 4 mark a transition. They resemble the gates to Macbeth's castle in Shakespeare's play, which in turn are like the gates of hell. However, they could also be seen as the gates of heaven, popularised in the expression 'the Pearly Gates'.

CONTEXT

'Larkin later claimed that he hadn't realised while writing the poem that he was using Longfellow's rhythms; in fact they are forcefully maintained until the final line, when their abandonment creates an apt sense of pathos, tilting the poem away from a world in which incident is pre-eminent to one in which emotion matters most' (Andrew Motion, *Philip Larkin: A Writer's Life*, p. 394).

CONTEXT

The *Hiawatha* metre is itself based on the Finnish epic the *Kalavala*.

The poem is unrhymed and is made up of three-line **stanzas**. The first four stanzas are in **trochaic tetrameter**, which is the often-parodied **metre** of Longfellow's poem *Hiawatha*, although nothing about Larkin's poem suggests parody. The metre consists of four metric **feet**, each consisting of two syllables, the first stressed, the second unstressed. It conveys a sense of driving force, suggesting the inevitability of the explosion. It also suggests the vigour of the men. So long as it runs smoothly, it creates a veneer of all being well, but in stanza 5 the metre breaks down, marking the explosion. It is resumed again in stanza 7, suggesting that the men's lives continue after death. The metre is again abandoned in the final line, emphasising its mystical and poignant message. Interestingly, the lines where the metre is lost contain the same number of syllables as the others, but differently stressed. For example in 'At <u>noon</u>, there <u>came</u> a <u>tremor</u>; <u>cows</u>', the sense demands that we emphasise the underlined words, making the line **iambic** rather than **trochaic**.

CHECK THE BOOK

D. H. Lawrence's novel *Sons and Lovers* (1913) contains a scene in which a pit disaster of this type occurs.

Larkin also uses **alliteration** to make the poem move along at a steady pace: 'the slagheap slept' (3); 'pitboots . . . pipe-smoke' (4–5); and 'larger than in life' (22). On the other hand, in the two stanzas that abandon the *Hiawatha* metre, he uses the technique of **enjambment** to signify disruption of this forward movement. This occurs in 'cows/ Stopped chewing', 'sun/ Scarfed as in a heat-haze' and 'they/ Are sitting . . .' (13–17).

GLOSSARY

2	**pithead** place directly above the mine from which miners would be lowered underground
3	**slagheap** heap of coal mining waste
10	**moleskins** skins of moles sewn into trousers

EXTENDED COMMENTARIES

LIVINGS

Uniquely in this collection, 'Livings' is a triptych (see **Critical history: Initial reception**) consisting of what are really three separate poems linked loosely by their theme. All three enter into a realm of characterisation and narrative more usually associated with fiction. The most obvious thematic link between them is, as the title suggests, that each one is about how people earn their livings. This is most true for the first two sections, the first focusing on the lonely life of the agricultural supplies salesman on his quarterly business trip to a slightly shabby hotel, and the second on the solitary (but not necessarily lonely) life of a lighthouse keeper. The third appears to describe a group of eighteenth-century Cambridge dons, or possibly clerics. There is no direct reference to their work, except that one of their topics of conversation is 'Which advowson [a paid clerical officer] looks the fairest' (III.5), and their shelves 'hold prayers and proofs' (III.22). However, they appear to be colleagues dining together.

Beyond the loose subject of work, the three sections explore one of Larkin's major themes – solitude with its risk of loneliness versus social interchange. The agricultural salesman does not admit to loneliness, but he is an outsider living a rather empty life. The lighthouse keeper chooses solitude: his only friends are mussels and limpets. The characters in the third section enjoy a social occasion, oiled by alcohol, but their conversation is fairly empty. For them, company is a distraction rather than a communion of souls.

Another link between the sections is the dynamic between change and stagnation. The salesman's evening is predictable and dull, and he ends by saying that 'It's time for change' (I.24); the lighthouse keeper seems to hide from a threatening world, resisting change, and consulting his divining-cards; and the characters in the third section are stuck in their ways. The 'Chaldean constellations' overhead (III.23) dwarf their habits and conversation and imply the existence of something cosmically enduring.

LIVINGS I

'Livings I' contains the clearest character delineation, not just in 'Livings' but in the whole of *High Windows*. The salesman's life is prosaic, but he has at least a hint of lyrical longing that makes him sense the emptiness of his life and admit that it is 'time for change' (24). He takes no great interest in his job, describing it in an offhand way: 'things like dips and feed' (1). His visit is habitual – 'Every third month' (2) and he finds himself 'wondering why/ I think it's worth while coming' (21–2). He is describing not a particular trip, but every trip – because they are all the same. As for the hotel, it

> **CONTEXT**
> 'Livings' was first published in the *Observer* newspaper.

> **CONTEXT**
> The opening line of 'Livings I' was spoken by a man named Saville Bradbury at a dinner attended by Larkin in 1971. Larkin said at the time, 'That would make a good first line of a poem'.

CONTEXT

Leaving dashes or blanks was a common way to avoid using a specific place name; the technique fits the 1929 setting of 'Livings I'. Nowadays a writer would be more likely to use a fictitious name.

could be any second-rate market town hotel, as suggested by the blanks. The 'One beer' (6) is a token gesture towards pleasure, and the dullness of 'the dinner' (6) is revealed by the phrase being placed in **ironic** quotation marks, suggesting that the meal hardly merits it. Nor does it merit more description than 'soup to stewed pears' (7), the **alliteration** serving to diminish and dismiss, as it does in 'Livings III' (for example, in 'prayers and proofs' [18]).

But dullness is only part of the picture. More important is that, despite his quarterly visits, the salesman remains an outsider. His 'lean old leather case' (4), compactly indicating the character of his life, and how long he has done this job, is carried 'up to a single' (5), emphasising his loneliness. Nor is there any mention of a wife at home. For lack of anything better to do, he reads the entire local paper, including the car adverts. Presumably the other characters, being locals, would eat at home, but he eats alone (like the lighthouse keeper in 'Livings II', but unlike the characters in 'Livings III'). In **stanza** 2, he joins in with local gossip of an impersonal financial nature, but there is no intimacy: he is not on first-name terms. The setting, with pictures that 'Nobody minds or notices' (16) has a stale familiarity. Perhaps a game of dominoes in the bar would be more entertaining. The salesman stands 'a round' (16), possibly to endear himself to the others, but there is also the double meaning of 'standing around', purposelessly.

Stanza 3 shifts in time and mood. There is a lyrical moment as the salesman, perhaps looking out of his window, notices 'a big sky' which 'Drains down the estuary like the bed/ Of a gold river' (17–19). This image – the only one in this section – seems to promise something bigger than the narrow confines of his life. However, it is worth noting that 'gold' suggests money (as in 'Solar') as well as evening light, and the Customs House, while lit up, is still a symbol of materialism and confinement.

 CHECK THE NET

For information on what the Customs and Excise (now called Revenue and Customs) department does, see **www.hmrc.gov.uk**

Brooding over this section is the shadow of external events. The mention of trenches in stanza 2 refers to the First World War, and the ex-Army sheets of stanza 3 remind us that the war was only eleven years earlier. Moreover, 1929 was the year of the Wall Street Crash, the trigger for the Depression, which hit British agriculture hard (some farmers are already 'taking the knock', [11]).

GLOSSARY

1	**dips**	liquid chemical preparations for the prevention of disease in farm animals, especially sheep
4	**boots**	hotel porter who would, among other menial tasks, clean guests' boots (cf. 'Boots' in Cinderella)
9	**Smoke Room**	room in a hotel or pub which was socially a cut above the bar. Also traditionally where men would smoke
11	**taking the knock**	suffering financial hardship
12	**stock**	cattle
16	**dominoes**	pub game played with wooden numbered pieces
	stand a round	buy drinks for those present
19	**Customs House**	in a port, the office of Customs and Excise, who would enforce the paying of customs duty on imports

CONTEXT

The Wall Street Crash in 1929 was the collapse of the US Stock Market. Investors panicked and sold their shares, causing businesses to collapse and personal bankruptcy on a huge scale. This was the start of the Depression, when people were reluctant to invest and business stagnated. This had a knock-on effect in Britain, and there was widespread unemployment. Agriculture was hard hit. The effects of the Depression, especially in Germany, helped to create social unrest, one of the major causes of the Second World War.

LIVINGS II

While the subject of 'Livings I' is a rather lonely character who attempts to make some sort of social contact, the lighthouse keeper of part II has deliberately isolated himself. Interestingly, the language of this section is far more consciously poetic than in the other two. In addition, there is a similarity between the lighthouse keeper and the **persona** of '*Vers de Société*'. The lighthouse keeper is 'Guarded by brilliance' (26): as long as his light shines, the outside world will leave him alone – by avoiding the lighthouse. The speaker in '*Vers de Société*' (or simply Larkin himself) would rather be alone 'Under a lamp, hearing the noise of wind' (15) than at a social event. Perhaps, then, the lighthouse keeper is the most like Larkin of the three personae, or at least the most poetic.

By contrast with 'Livings I', this section is dynamic and linguistically colourful. It is full of energetic verbs: the sea 'explodes upwards/ Relapsing, to slaver' (2–3), the rocks 'writhe' (6), the shellfish 'Husband their tenacity' (8). Vigorous descriptive phrases such as 'freezing slither' (9), 'Grape-dark' (12), 'wind-shuttered' (17) and 'Leather-black' (25) bring the lighthouse keeper's experience vividly to life, as do his three exclamations:

> Running suds, rejoice! (5)
> Creatures, I cherish you! (10)
> Keep it all off! (21)

 CHECK THE NET

For information on lighthouses, go to **www.trinityhouse. co.uk** and click on Aids to Navigation, then Lighthouses. This page reveals that the UK's last manned lighthouse was automated in 1998.

CONTEXT

The phrase 'Grape-dark', describing the sky, is reminiscent of Homer, who in the *Odyssey* often uses the phrase 'wine-dark sea'. 'Leather-black', describing the sea, recalls Dylan Thomas (1914–53), a poet whom Larkin admired, at least in his youth. In his play for radio *Under Milk Wood*, Thomas describes the town as 'starless and bible-black', leading to the 'sloe black, slow, black, crow black fishing boat-bobbing sea'.

QUESTION
What do you think is symbolised by the liners groping westwards? Is it the threat of change, death, or simply a world which the lighthouse keeper cannot comprehend?

In 'Livings I', the only imagery comes in **stanza** 3; 'Livings II' is a feast of imagery. In addition to the phrases already quoted, we find the sea described as the 'salt/ Unsown stirring fields' (12–13), the radio 'rubs its legs' (14) – perhaps like crickets or grasshoppers – the fleets are 'pent like hounds' (18), the inns are 'humped' like people resisting the wind (19), and the maritime pictures on the inn walls are 'kippered' (smoked) by their fires (20).

Rhythmically, 'Livings II' is also very different from the other sections. Short, mostly **dactylic** lines, the emphasis often falling on the first syllable of the line (as in the first line), create a terse vigour which is heightened by the use of **alliteration**, as in 'snow swerves' (stanza 5). While the salesman of the first section is an ordinary (if lonely), relatively transparent character, the lighthouse keeper is enigmatically passionate. Above all, he has chosen solitude. The outside world is simply an 'elsewhere' (15) significant only insofar as it leaves him alone. If the pressure is dropping ('Barometers falling', [16]), leading to stormy weather, and ships are 'pent like hounds' ([18], prevented by bad weather from going to sea), that suits him.

Larkin makes an interesting inversion in having the lighthouse keeper describe himself as being guarded by the light, rather than the light protecting others. Larkin uses light **ambiguously** in this collection. Often it is, paradoxically, somehow darkened, as it is in 'Livings I' by the smoke of the Smoke Room. In 'Friday Night in the Royal Station Hotel', which describes a lonely, isolated place and therefore has something in common with parts I and II, the light 'spreads darkly downwards' (1). In 'Livings II' the light is brilliant, but its main function is to ensure the lighthouse keeper's isolation, **symbolised** by his single 'plate and spoon' (27).

There is also light in the poem's strange ending. The liners' rows of lit-up windows are 'Lit shelved' (29), but in the outer darkness they 'Grope like mad worlds westward' (last line). They are travelling in the direction of the New World and the setting sun, and, by traditional association, death.

GLOSSARY	
3	**slaver** allow saliva to run from the mouth (like a hungry dog)
4	**landing-stage** a concrete pier below the lighthouse from which to disembark from a boat
7	**Mussels, limpets** types of shellfish which cling to rock
16	**Barometers falling** a barometer is a device to measure air pressure. Falling air pressure would indicate the approach of unsettled weather
28	**divining-cards** playing cards used for the purpose of fortune-telling; probably Tarot cards

CONTEXT

The image of the fleets 'pent like hounds' in 'Livings II', stanza 4, reminds us that Larkin was strongly opposed to blood sports.

LIVINGS III

The **narrator** in this section is a relatively shadowy figure compared with the salesman and the lighthouse keeper. He appears to be a college don or cleric, possibly living in the eighteenth century, but the conversation he enjoys with his colleagues, while wide-ranging, is hardly elevated. They discuss colleagues' prospects ('which advowson looks the fairest' [5]), commerce, women's sexual organs and the connection between Judas and a hangman who was himself hanged for murder. As 'the wine heats temper' (13), their opinions range over a list of subjects which are connected only by **alliteration** – a technique which Larkin uses elsewhere, for example in 'Livings I' and in 'Show Saturday', to make light of listed items. The effect is to show that the discussion, though lively, is seemingly random and therefore fairly superficial.

The tone of the narration, too, is lively but casual, and this is reinforced by the glibly regular rhyme scheme (ABAB, CDCD, etc.) and rhythm, which borders on **doggerel**. The mood, more rugby club than academia, is no doubt encouraged by the absence of 'the Master' (1), which encourages heavier drinking and relaxation ('Topics are raised with no less ease' [4], is an understatement). The parenthesised comment on his absence **ironically** mocks his reasons for absence, in the tone of schoolboys mocking their teacher. The placing of a 'jordan' behind a screen to save 'going to the bogs' (11) adds to the rather coarse male mood. These details help to create the archaic setting, as does the phrase 'The wine heats temper and complexion' (13). Other than this, however, the language is modern.

 CHECK THE BOOK

For the 'nocturnal vapours' which the Master wishes to avoid, see Shakespeare's *Julius Caesar*, in which Portia asks: *'What, is Brutus sick/ And will he steal out of his wholesome bed/ To dare the vile contagion of the night,/ And tempt the rheumy and unpurged air/ To add unto his sickness?'* (II.1.265–9).

CHECK THE BOOK

The regularity of **metre** and rhyme in 'Livings III' is reminiscent of W. H. Auden. For example, see 'Stephano' (written in the voice of a character from Shakespeare's *The Tempest*), which has the same rhyme scheme and a similar metre. Auden also uses the technique of building up an overall picture with glimpses of apparently unconnected scenes, as in 'The Fall of Rome'. Both poems are contained in Auden's *Selected Poems* (Faber, 1968).

CONTEXT

Larkin went to Oxford University, not Cambridge, but both were steeped in the same sort of traditions, which included the drinking of port.

The final **stanza** quietly abandons the narrator, picturing more than he could practically observe. It leads us through a cinematic series of images, cutting between seemingly unconnected scenes to form an overall picture – the fields, the street, the poor student shivering alone in his study, the cat. With the clock bells which 'discuss the hour's gradation' (21), echoing the human discussion, we return to the college and its 'prayers and proofs' (22) again, linked by **alliteration** to suggest their equal unimportance. Finally, we are drawn up from the petty human world to something more grand and enduring – the constellations overhead, just as they were when first named by Chaldean astronomers. The effect is something like that of 'High Windows', 'Money' and 'The Card-Players': the mundane gives way in the end to something more remarkable.

GLOSSARY	
2	**Nocturnal vapours** night air, at one time thought to be damaging to the health
3	**port** a fortified wine popular in colleges and traditionally passed around in one direction only
5	**advowson** a paid clerical post
6	**Snape** a place name, perhaps referring to a real place in Suffolk
7	*pudendum mulieris* Latin for, literally, 'the shameful thing of a woman'
8	**Judas like Jack Ketch** Judas, in the New Testament, betrayed Christ and then hanged himself. Jack Ketch was a hangman hanged for murder in 1718; he therefore in a sense betrayed his profession
10	**Starveling** a name, perhaps suggesting that, as a servant, he dines less well than his masters. This is also the name of one of the rougher, comic characters in *A Midsummer Night's Dream*
11	**jordan** a slang term for a commode or portable toilet
15	**rheumy fevers** fevers causing mucous discharge from the eyes or nose; at one time associated with night air
19	**sizar** a poor student paid to do menial tasks around the college (a term used at Cambridge and Trinity College, Dublin)
23	**Chaldean** an ancient Semitic people living in Babylonia sa to be learned in astronomy

VERS DE SOCIÉTÉ

This poem, more than any other in the collection, focuses on Larkin's ambivalent attitude towards company, his longing for solitude, and his fear of loneliness. It moves between **irony** and lyricism, and presents a very personal voice, as Larkin scrutinises his feelings. However, it is also universal in appeal, highlighting as it does the necessary balance between the personal and the social which we must all achieve.

The poem begins with a sharply **satirised** invitation, and the narrator's intended rejection of it. However, it continues with the narrator at first dismissing social contact as a meaningless waste of time, extolling the joys of solitude, but then reluctantly acknowledging a need for company – if only to block out troubling thoughts, perhaps of mortality.

The mocking title means 'Social Verse', but specifically refers to a tradition of light, witty verse written to entertain sophisticated though possibly shallow audiences. It hints at his expectation of social events being a waste of time, as is made clear by the ironic wording of the invitation in the first three lines, and the tersely vulgar way in which it is declined.

Despite this rejection and the solitary appeal of the 'breathing' gas fire and 'the trees . . . darkly swayed' (5), Larkin admits that it is hard to be alone. He is cruelly dismissive of the female conversation offered in stanza 2, of the time 'that has flown/ Straight into nothingness by being filled/ With forks and faces' (12–14); as in 'Livings', the **alliteration** underlines the dismissal. He even dismisses his host's sherry as only fit for 'washing' with (9). Conversely, he presents solitude as a refinement of one's sensibilities, in which one observes 'the moon thinned/ To an air-sharpened blade' (16–17). This is 'a life' (18), as opposed to the living death of having to socialise with people with whom one has not chosen to spend time. Significantly, the social contact represented is of the almost inevitably shallow variety – not friendship, and not even on first-name terms. 'Warlock-Williams' (6) is a double-barrelled surname. It may also imply that, for the poet, socialising is akin to ritual witchcraft. This may also mean

CHECK THE NET

Go to **www.answers.com** for a note on the kind of verse known as *Vers de Société* (type 'vers de société' into the search box). It also gives a link to a page on Ogden Nash, a twentieth-century exponent of this type of verse.

WWW. CHECK THE NET
To find out about *Which* magazine as it is now, see www.which.co.uk

CONTEXT
On the subject of how we treat others, W. H. Auden (1907–73) wrote in his poem 'September 1, 1939', 'We must love one another or die.'

that the choice of *Which* magazine is intended as a pun – even though it refers to a consumer magazine.

In **stanza** 4, however, the **narrator** comments on the popular rejection of solitude, and of the ideal of the hermit – a figure who in ancient times commanded respect for his rejection of human company in favour of a life of introspective contemplation. The hermit, says the narrator, cannot be communing with God, because God is dead. Instead, he says, we want people to be 'nice' to us, 'which means/ Doing it back somehow' (22–3). The bland vagueness of the language reveals Larkin's scepticism, but he is still left with a dilemma which he cannot resolve. As in 'To the Sea', he considers the possibility that social ritual is the best we can manage. Here, it is 'Playing at goodness, like going to church' (25) when there is no God. He wonders if we should make the effort, paying lip-service to an idea of kindness ('Asking that ass about his fool research' [27] – one thinks of Jake Balokowsky in 'Posterity') but he can reach no conclusion ('Oh hell' [30]). As in 'To the Sea', Larkin seems to flounder slightly in his thinking, but perhaps because this simply reflects his own uncertainty about how we should behave. He seems to think that perhaps we should at least 'try to feel' benevolent towards others, because it 'shows us what should be' (28–9), as if by making a pretence of virtue we could actually find ourselves developing the real thing. But then he dismisses even that as 'too subtle . . . Too decent' (30); intellectualism and falling back on bourgeois good form are at best confusing, so that he gives up on the debate.

The last stanza suggests that only the young can be alone without being troubled by troubling thoughts of mortality. 'The time is shorter now for company' (32), so one must seize it while there is still time. The light makes solitude possible, as it does for the lighthouse keeper in 'Livings II', but it barely holds at bay the gloomy thoughts that lurk, **personified**, whispering from our unconscious just beyond it. Perhaps, then, light **symbolises** the conscious mind here.

The **metre** of the poem is basically **iambic pentameter**, which makes it move along quite smoothly, but the fourth line of each stanza is short, which Larkin uses especially in stanzas 4 and 6 to create a pause for thought. The rhyme scheme reflects the overall structure of the poem. The first and last stanzas, in which the poet first begins to decline, and then accepts, the invitation, are composed of simple rhyming couplets. Each of the intervening stanzas, however, in which the poet deliberates the solitude/company dilemma, has a different and more complex rhyme scheme: stanza 2 is ABBCCA, stanza 3 is ABCCBA, stanza 4 is ABBCAC, and stanza 5 is ABACCB. This reflects the subtle twists of thought as the dilemma is explored.

GLOSSARY		
6	**Warlock** a male witch	
9	**washing sherry** cheap sherry, like 'cooking wine'	

SHOW SATURDAY

It is worth noting that this was the last poem in *High Windows* to be written, and that Larkin particularly wanted to include it to give the collection more substance. It is a wonderful celebration of community. It is also unusual in the collection, as it presents what is at least superficially a simple narrative, describing a rural show from fairly early on to its finish. Larkin observes the whole procedure with a certain detachment, uncritically, and even with affection. Most of the poem is devoted to recording the details of the show. Only in the penultimate stanza does he comment on those who take part, and only in the final stanza on the overall significance of the event, socially and in terms of the seasonal round.

The poem has been described by Andrew Motion (in *Philip Larkin: A Writer's Life*) as celebrating 'pastoral pleasures that seem "ordinary" but are in fact ancient and sanctioned by custom'. It is 'a huge hymn to old England' that 'ends in a prayer'. As Motion also comments, the poem links to a number of other Larkin poems which celebrate a sense of community. The title poem of *The Whitsun Weddings* is one of these, and 'To the Sea', in this collection, is another. The England described is also the same rather idealised one that Larkin sorrowfully anticipates losing in 'Going, Going'.

CONTEXT

The scene described in 'Show Saturday' is Bellingham Show in Northumberland, which Larkin visited most years with his girlfriend Monica Jones. The two wrestlers are the Harrington Brothers, who appeared every year. As Monica would recognise all this, one could read a romantic purpose into the poem, and even a secondary meaning into its final sentence: 'Let it always be there.'

Larkin goes into a great deal of detail in this poem, closely observing the scene in a slightly detached and almost uncomprehending way, as if it arouses his interest, even his affection, but still baffles him. For example, the ponies are 'dragged to and fro for/ Bewildering requirements' (37–8) and the precise purpose of the 'man with pound notes round his hat/ And a lit up board' (9–10) is something of a mystery. The **enjambment** between some of the **stanzas** creates a sense not only of the show sprawling, but of the observer wandering from one part of it to another, although the rhyme scheme (ABACBDCD) helps to hold the poem together, perhaps hinting at social cohesion.

At the outset, the poet expresses a traditional English concern for the weather. It is a grey day, but the show's supporters are undeterred, as revealed by the number of cars jamming the lanes. Larkin then breaks into the first of several lists, each item followed by a parenthesised comment. He evidently knows enough to observe exactly how dog owners attempt to show off their dogs to their best advantage, to know why the owners of the ponies stroke their manes, what the breeds of sheep are, and the cause of the 'squealing logs' (5). **Alliteration** is used for appeal, rather than as a means of dismissal as in 'Vers de Société': 'keen crowd', 'judges . . . jeep . . . jumping' (6–8). The **assonance** in this line – 'meet by a jeep' – helps to create a sense of social harmony.

The second stanza, beginning mid-sentence, provides a medley of attractions: the pound note man, and the 'Bead-stalls, balloon-men, a Bank; a beer-marquee' (11). Here the alliteration is, again, appealing and produces a sense of proliferation. It seems that everyone is catered for, as this is a truly communal experience. Basic human needs are represented by the Gents (perhaps like the jordan in 'Livings III'). The word 'Folks' (13) suggests the 'folksiness' of the event – it is the opposite of elitist. The **simile** which describes the bales as being 'Like great straw dice' (13) is unremarkable (compared with some of Larkin's other images), but perhaps alludes to another traditional pastime, as well as the element of chance in the event. The importance of community is emphasised by the fact that this is one of only two poems in *High Windows* in which Larkin even mentions children (the other is 'To the Sea'). Here they are 'freed' by the event to 'scrap' (15), ignored by their parents.

CONTEXT

The VPA (Village Produce Association) is a time-honoured institution even now in many villages. Members compare notes on growing techniques and hold competitions.

Stanza 3 is devoted to the wrestling, a traditional pastime going back at least as far as medieval fairs. Larkin pictures the scene, its elements receding from the central focus point ('people, then cars;/ Then trees; then pale sky'), then switches back to the slightly absurd spectacle of the 'young men in acrobats' tights/ And embroidered trunks' (20–1). Their hugging could almost be affectionate rather than combative, and their movements seem solid rather than aggressive or even slick. Indeed the lack of aggression is shown in their being 'not so much fights/ As long immobile strainings' [21–2]). The image of 'a two-man scrum' (20) is no more remarkable than that of the dice in the previous stanza, but it is appropriate to the occasion.

In stanza 4 we move to 'the long high tent of growing and making' (25), where the village vegetable produce and handicrafts are displayed. Here, Larkin shows a familiarity with the language of village produce competitions. Such phrases as 'six pods of/ Broad beans (one split open)' (27–8), 'four brown eggs, four white eggs,/ Four plain scones, four dropped scones' (30–1) are typical of the wording of the specified competition categories. (The entries have to be displayed exactly as described.) Larkin admires the 'recession of skills' (32), perhaps meaning that behind each skill lies another: behind the skill of arranging scones lies that of baking them, behind that the skill of the flour-maker, and so on. It is interesting to note, too, that the semi-religious social ritual nature of the competition is indicated in the simile comparing the leeks with 'church candles' (27).

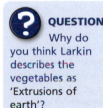

QUESTION
Why do you think Larkin describes the vegetables as 'Extrusions of earth'?

Larkin's admiration for the gardening, cookery and handicraft skills – 'all worthy, all well done' (33) – seems sincere, and it is emphasised by the repetition of 'all'. Nonetheless, he undercuts this slightly by commenting that the honeycombs are even more worthy. This is presumably a compliment to the bees, unless by 'less', Larkin is referring to price. (Whereas the cookery would be for the competition, the handicrafts would probably be for sale.)

Moving outside the tent, Larkin begins to wind up the show. Already 'the jumping's over' (34), leaving the ring to younger riders. Here, Larkin gives us another of his lists, describing the various baffling demands made on the ponies (which they nevertheless do not mind). It is with the phrase 'But now, in the

CONTEXT

Shakespeare in *As You Like It* wrote: 'All the world's a stage,/ And all the men and women merely players:/ They have their exits and their entrances;/ And one man in his time plays many parts . . .' (II.7.139–42).

CHECK THE BOOK

The description of the 'types' in the penultimate stanza of 'Show Saturday' is reminiscent of Dylan Thomas, especially Larkin's 'watchful as weasels'. This is perhaps because the phrase owes more to its musical **alliterative** quality than to precise observation. See, for example, Thomas' poetic prose in *A Child's Christmas in Wales* (1955).

background' (38) that we really see the show start to draw to a close. The description of the horse-boxes as being 'Like shifting scenery' (39) is theatrical, but also brings to mind Shakespeare's comment that 'All the world's a stage'. It makes us realise that in a sense the entire show is a construct. The community that it conjures is temporary, even if it is based on a community that exists in a broader sense, taking in the 'far-off farms' (41) and 'private addresses' (43) of the next **stanza**.

In stanza 6 we move to a key contrast in the poem, between the communal, or social, world and the private. They are linked but not the same. In this stanza we have a sense of the show, and its community, dispersing. People return to their own homes, in individual, rather lonely-sounding 'high stone one-street villages' (44). The individual 'sports finals' (45) newspapers stuck in their doors, and their individual allotments, underline the contrast.

There is also a movement, from the end of stanza 6 onwards, from the 'ended husk/ Of summer' (47–8) to autumn and 'To winter coming' (57). This is matched by the way in which Larkin now begins to describe those attending the show in more detail, hinting at their individuality, though doing it by describing types: 'wool-defined women' (49), middle-class county women in tight sweaters, children proud of their competitive riding achievements ('all saddle-swank', [50]), the unflatteringly described 'mugfaced middleaged wives' (50), the husbands, the sons. All the family is here, but they are all returning to their ordinary private 'local lives' (53). However, these still contain social elements: 'loud occasions/ In the Corn Exchange' and 'market days in bars' (55–6).

The final stanza soberly reminds us of approaching winter and the show's recession into the more humdrum workaday world, but it also turns into the nearest Larkin ever gets to a prayer, a heart-felt wish, even an exhortation. He wants the sense of community contained in the show to 'stay hidden there like strength' (59), beneath petty materialism. He wants it, simply, to remain 'something people do' (60), not noticing, and therefore in a way defeating, the ravages of time, and of mortality – 'how time's rolling smithy-smoke/ Shadows much greater gestures' (61). The rather grandiose **personification** of time as a blacksmith is unusual for Larkin (and is more like Auden), but it lends an appropriate grandeur to the homage he is paying to the social ritual of the show. For Larkin, it is an ancestral community linking all those who take part, and all those who have ever taken part. Like the turning of the year itself, it offers healing – 'Regenerate union' (56). Larkin's final sentence is both humble and moving in its simplicity.

CONTEXT

Other poets have personified time in various ways, for example Andrew Marvell, in 'To His Coy Mistress', wrote: 'But at my back I always hear/ Time's winged chariot hurrying near.'

GLOSSARY	
5	**Cheviot and Blackface** northern varieties of sheep
31	**plain scones . . . dropped scones** small cakes of flour, fat and milk either shaped in a baking tray (plain) or 'dropped' straight on to a hotplate.
36	**Musical Stalls** like musical chairs, but on horseback. Contestants ride their ponies round a ring to music. When the music stops, they have to steer their pony into a makeshift 'stall'. There is one fewer stall than the number of contestants. Each time the music restarts, a stall is removed
49	**hunters** horses used for fox-hunting
56	**Corn Exchange** building in a market town in which corn was traditionally traded

QUESTION
What 'much greater gestures' do you think are shadowed by 'time's rolling smithy-smoke' in the final stanza of 'Show Saturday'?

PART THREE

CRITICAL APPROACHES

THEMES

YOUTH, AGE AND MORTALITY

Larkin was only fifty-two when *High Windows* was published, yet it is dominated by an overriding sense of lost youth, time passing and the imminence of death. Even in poems not ostensibly concerned with these themes, they are often implied. 'Sympathy in White Major' is principally about self-image and the disappointments of public life, yet in it the poet takes on the **persona** of someone toasting him after his death, as if Larkin were penning his own obituary. 'Posterity', too, hints at how Larkin might be remembered, thanks to a reluctant biographer. Even in 'The Card-Players' death lurks in Old Prijck's 'skull face' (7). In 'Going, Going', Larkin is concerned with the disappearance of the England he has known, but one aspect of this concern is that it will have gone even before Larkin himself has died. In other poems, the concerns of youth, age and mortality are far more explicit. Although some of the poems focus on youth, some on aging, and some on death, in a sense all these can be subsumed into the single fact of mortality.

CHECK THE BOOK

One of many poems commenting on the loss of young life in the trenches is Siegfried Sassoon's 'Suicide in the Trenches' (1917).

Even when Larkin writes about nature, it is often in terms of the transitory. 'Cut Grass' apparently laments the mowing of the grass, but this is really a **metaphor** for human life, as frail and brief as the grass. His description of its being cut down in early summer is reminiscent of First World War poetry describing the loss of young men in the trenches. 'The Trees' is even more **ambiguous**. The trees appear to offer consolation in the face of our inevitable aging, yet 'Their greenness is a kind of grief' (4) and their seeming annual renewal is only a 'trick of looking new' (7): beneath their renewed greenery the trees are actually aging. Nor does Larkin seem convinced that it is possible to 'Begin afresh, afresh, afresh' (12) as they do. In 'The Card-Players', on the other hand, the 'century-wide trees' (10) provide a temporal contrast with the short lives of the drinkers. In a similar way, 'Solar' compares the constancy of the sun with the recurring nature of human needs.

A number of the poems refer to the passing of time, which is an aspect of mortality. Sometimes this is historical, as in 'Livings I', which ends with the statement 'It's time for change, in nineteen twenty-nine' (24) or 'Annus Mirabilis', in which the starting point of sexual intercourse is precisely dated. At other times, as in 'Livings III', 'Friday Night in the Royal Station Hotel' and 'The Building', we are given a sense of the hours passing. Most tellingly, however, in '*Vers de Société*', the poet expresses resentment at the wasting of time, although this is placed in the context of his aging: 'The time is shorter now for company' (32).

Several poems refer explicitly to the youth which Larkin so clearly feels is behind him. In 'How Distant', the young men are seen as an active force, pursuing opportunities not yet lost, enjoying the adventure of travel and the imagined possibilities inspired by the sight of a girl doing her laundry. Significantly, the poem links power – the 'Assumption of the startled century' (16) – with the ability to make choices, and with creativity, and freedom:

> The huge decisions printed out by feet
> Inventing where they tread. (18–19)

In the final **stanza** of 'Sad Steps' Larkin seems to long for his lost youth, although he realises that 'being young' involves pain, and he takes some consolation in the fact that youth is 'for others undiminished somewhere' (18). However, in 'High Windows' itself youth is seen as holding out false promise. The sexual freedom enjoyed by modern youth is only **ironically** referred to as 'paradise/ Everyone old has dreamed of all their lives' (4–5).

Other poems focus on old age. 'To the Sea' touches on this, when we see the middle-aged pushing the old in wheelchairs so that they can enjoy a last summer before death. Larkin's most arresting view of old age, however, comes in 'The Old Fools'. Some have seen the poem as lacking in sympathy for the elderly, but at least it contemplates the worst of old age without flinching. It involves the physical ignomy of drooling and incontinence, but also a frightening loss of mental powers, including the inability to remain in touch with the present or even to realise what is going on. The old people's 'thin, continuous dreaming' (10) is half-way to death.

 **CHECK THE FILM**

Iris (2001), directed by Richard Eyre and starring Judi Dench, Jim Broadbent and Kate Winslet, is a biography of Iris Murdoch, showing her gradual loss of her mental faculties through Alzheimer's disease. This is reminiscent of 'The Old Fools'.

Larkin speculates with quiet horror rather than compassion on what it must be like to find people and places only vaguely and bafflingly familiar at best. The worst of it is, however, that they now live with 'the power/ Of choosing gone' (21–2). For Larkin, living life fully involves the freedom to make choices. The young have it, as in 'How Distant', but the 'old fools' have lost it altogether.

Some of the poems focus relentlessly on death itself. 'Dublinesque' is clearly about death in that it narrates a funeral procession, yet its mourners celebrate the life of the deceased, and even dance a few steps. Moreover, their shared grief brings them together in 'great friendliness' (13) and the memory of the deceased evokes both love and beauty.

'The Old Fools' also looks at death itself as the inevitable conclusion of old age. Larkin sees no hope here for an afterlife:

> At death, you break up: the bits that were you
> Start speeding away from each other for ever
> With no one to see. (13–15)

The 'old fools' are unaware of the awful imminence of death, 'Extinction's alp' (41), because they are too close to it to see it. For us it is a peak overshadowing us; for them it is 'rising ground' (44) because they are already climbing it.

The final poem of the collection, 'The Explosion', explores a very different kind of death – a sudden one. The miners are cut off in their prime, like the grass in 'Cut Grass', but at least they avoid the grim decline of the 'old fools'. This poem also, unusually for Larkin, hints at the possibility of an afterlife, but perhaps only in the memory of those left behind.

However, the poem which most chillingly focuses on death is 'The Building'. Those who wait in the hall, perhaps to have X-rays or tests, sit 'tamely' (9), already part-institutionalised, choice already partly gone (like the 'old fools'), and passive like a priest's congregation. Most are 'at that vague age that claims/ The end of choice' (20–1). When someone is fetched away, the rest 'cough, or glance below/ Seats' (16–17) in an awkward attempt to distract

CHECK THE BOOK

In Ian McEwan's *Saturday* (Vintage, 2005), there is a poignant scene in which the main character, Perowne, visits his mother in a nursing home. She no longer knows who he is.

themselves from reality, and they only look at each other to guess ailments, not to communicate (stanza 5). The approach of death is a series of rooms 'each one further off/ And harder to return from' (35–6). Those waiting 'know they are going to die' (57). The hospital can 'transcend/ The thought of dying' but not death itself. Nor can death be placated by the 'wasteful, weak, propitiatory flowers' brought by visitors to the sick and dying in the last line.

Larkin, then, is very much concerned with the transitory in all its aspects. He regrets the passing of his own youth and contemplates old age, the inevitability of death, and human fear of death, with honesty and detailed self-examination.

RELIGION AND RITUAL

The combined theme of religion and ritual emerges in *High Windows* in a number of ways. Larkin makes it clear that he is an atheist, but one for whom conventional religion might have given life a sense of purpose. At times he refers to religion directly, for example in '*Vers de Société*', in which he says:

> No one now
> Believes the hermit with his gown and dish
> Talking to God (who's gone too). (19–21)

In 'The Explosion', he quotes a biblical verse as if believing in its message himself:

> *The dead go on before us, they*
> *Are sitting in God's house in comfort,*
> *We shall see them face to face* – (16–18)

Although Larkin seems moved by the death of the miners, and by the vision which apparently occurred to their wives and loved ones, he does not really believe in the truth of the vision, however. Larkin uses italics to indicate that this is another voice, not his own comment. We also know from his other writings that he was an atheist. In the poem 'High Windows', religion is seen as something which was a source of guilt and restriction to the older generation, and which is now better left behind.

CHECK THE BOOK

The receding hospital rooms of 'The Building' resemble the rooms in Thomas Hardy's poem 'A Wasted Illness', in which he speaks of passing 'Through vaults of pain', past 'webby waxing things', until he comes to death's door, before making a recovery: 'And back slid I/ Along the galleries by which I came.' Larkin may have had this poem in mind; he certainly read Hardy and admitted to being influenced by him.

In 'The Old Fools', one of Larkin's darkest poems, he makes clear his belief that death is the end of everything. He anticipates death as being simply oblivion, an oblivion which is partly desired, as in his earlier poem 'Wants' ('Beneath it all, desire of oblivion runs'), but which on the whole fills him with foreboding. This fear is expressed in 'The Old Fools' when he refers to death as 'Extinction's alp' (41), but it is nowhere more clearly expressed than in 'The Building'. Here, the hospital is presented as a modern cathedral, our only hope in the face of death. It is 'a struggle to transcend/ The thought of dying' (60–1). The locked church in **stanza** 6 **symbolises** the death of God. The flowers brought by the relatives of the terminally ill are powerless to please a God who no longer exists, nor death itself.

In several poems, Larkin suggests that all we can grasp at now in place of religion is social ritual. 'To the Sea' presents the family seaside visit as a social ritual which has value in itself. '*Vers de Société*' recalls social events, including trying to be nice to others in the hope that they will be nice to you, 'Playing at goodness, like going to church' (25). Yet Larkin also seems to feel that perhaps observing the social rituals can somehow make us better people. He is undecided about this.

'Dublinesque' is one poem in which Larkin gives a religious social ritual, a funeral procession, a positive slant. Here, death has brought people together in a ritual that reinforces a positive sense of community, producing friendliness as well as sadness. 'Show Saturday', however, is the poem in which Larkin most clearly makes a religion of social ritual. His **simile** comparing leeks to church candles (stanza 4) shows the connection. At the end, moreover, Larkin offers up what is almost a prayer that such ancestral social rituals may continue for ever.

Nature, too, is an important force in some of the poems. Larkin is not a poet for whom nature is a religion, as it was for Wordsworth. Nor is he someone who wishes to explore the raw essence of nature in depth, like Ted Hughes. However, there are poems in which nature in a sense takes the place of religion. It gives a feeling of continuity, of things going on in a seasonal round, to some extent overcoming the threat of mortality. 'Show Saturday' does this, with

CHECK THE BOOK

Romantic poet William Wordsworth (1770–1850) often wrote about the spirit of nature, for example in *The Prelude*, where he addresses:
'*Ye presences of Nature in the sky And on the earth!/ Ye visions of the hills!/ And souls of lonely places!*'.

its mention of the seasons. 'The Trees' does so too, presenting the coming into leaf of the trees each year as a sign of hope. At the end of 'Forget What Did', the natural and celestial occurrences offer comfort in the face of personal suffering. In 'Livings III', the stars overhead offer, if not comfort, then a sense of cosmic grandeur that dwarfs personal suffering.

There are times, however, when Larkin moves beyond social ritual as a substitute for religion, to a sense of something more spiritual. In 'The Old Fools', he celebrates life as a 'million-petalled flower' (18). Most tellingly, at the end of 'High Windows' itself, he adopts the deep blue air of the sky as a symbol of something indefinable, something which 'shows/ Nothing, and is nowhere, and is endless' (20), but which perhaps on some mystical level represents oblivion without extinction – the consolation of something universal enduring beyond the end of the individual life.

ENGLISHNESS

While English national identity is not Larkin's most important theme, it is arguably the one for which he is best known. It has also made him a somewhat controversial figure, partly because of the racist and more generally right-wing tendencies revealed in his private correspondence, but also because of his leanings towards nationalism. These could be seen as limiting his vision to a relatively small arena, rather than allowing him to embrace universal truths. It does not help his reputation that his father was a known Nazi sympathiser, even during the war, and that Larkin himself could never entirely condemn Nazism (see **Background: Philip Larkin's life and work**).

Larkin's poetry offers no acknowledgement of Britain's multicultural society, but nor is it racist in any obvious way. It is also important that, while it is specifically English traditions that he celebrates (not even British ones in a wider sense), he does not claim that England is better than other countries. The possible exception to this is 'Homage to a Government' (see below).

Tom Paulin has written of Larkin, 'He journeys into the interior, into the unknown heart – the maybe missing centre – of Englishness' (*Guardian Unlimited* website). For Larkin, this heart

CHECK THE BOOK

For some, ritual is by definition meaningless. However, others such as Murry Hope see it as a means of achieving change by focusing one's mind. See her *The Psychology of Ritual* (Element Books, 1988).

CHECK THE NET

Tom Paulin is quoted on the *Guardian*'s Larkin page, which has a succinct summary of critical views on Larkin. Go to **http://books. guardian.co.uk**, click on Authors and follow the link to Larkin.

is rooted more than anywhere in tradition and social ritual. The two poems in which he expresses his feeling for Englishness most clearly are 'Going, Going' and 'Show Saturday'. In 'Going, Going', the more negative of the two, Larkin regrets the rapid loss of much of what he considers to be quintessentially English: 'The shadows, the meadows, the lanes,/ The guildhalls, the carved choirs' (45–6). He blames this loss on the materialistic greed of big business, but he also implies that the lower classes are in part responsible because of their clamouring demands for more of everything. Lower-class village youths are an acceptable part of English tradition only as long as they remain in their place – climbing trees. He also talks rather vaguely about pollution, but his failure to identify this as a global problem does seem to be rather limited – even for the 1970s.

'Show Saturday' is a more positive, more self-assured, and better-informed poem, based on close personal observation in a way that 'Going, Going' is not. In it, Larkin describes a country show, a rural tradition which has carried on for hundreds of years. The poem has a depth to it which goes beyond the appreciation of mere longevity of tradition. He sees this tradition as bringing about a sense of community which continues to lie dormant even after the individuals who have attended the show have returned to their private addresses and their workaday lives. He also admires the traditional skills which are demonstrated at the show. He seems to regard this manifestation of Englishness as something which endures in the face of individual mortality.

'To the Sea' is related to 'Going, Going' in that it celebrates a traditional English pastime – though one which is less deep-rooted than the country show and involves no traditional skills. However, it does celebrate the observance of social ritual, which in 'Going, Going' expressly stands in place of religion.

Part of Larkin's love of Englishness is his affection for the English countryside and this appears in two of the poems in 'High Windows'. In 'The Trees' there is an appreciation of nature, though the emphasis is more on using the trees as a **metaphor** for regeneration. His affection for the English countryside is more apparent in 'Cut Grass', where his naming of particular species of tree and plant gives the poem a depth lacking in 'The Trees'. The mention of Queen Anne's lace, a flowering plant, also suggests a sense of English history.

The theme of Englishness arises more controversially in 'Homage to a Government'. This poem, written in response to Labour Prime Minister Harold Wilson's decision to bring home all British troops from east of Suez, borders on jingoism in a way that Larkin's other poems never do. This poem could be seen as mourning the loss of empire, as if Britain is more civilised than other countries, and should therefore be guarding them or keeping them in order. The poem puts forward a rather disingenuous argument that we should be keeping troops abroad because by not doing so we are saving money – as if the only reason for bringing them home is that we can no longer afford to keep them there, and that this is in some way shameful. Larkin was not a particularly astute political commentator, and this poem is more to be regarded for its comment on materialism than for its politics.

A number of other poems in *High Windows* explore the theme of Englishness in terms of the national character. The rather mournful and reserved agricultural salesman in 'Livings I' is in some ways typically English, as is the impersonal male conversation in the Smoke Room. Even the fact that there is a Smoke Room, as distinct from the Bar, is evidence of the British class system. The insularity of the lighthouse keeper in 'Livings II' could be seen as a national characteristic of this island nation. There is also something more darkly English in the quiet social restraint and denial of death demonstrated in 'The Building'. This is in contrast to the way in which death brings people together in 'Dublinesque'. The nation's tendency towards sexual inhibition, lampooned in the long-running comic play by Alistair Foot and Anthony Marriott, *No Sex Please, We're British*, is revealed in 'Annus Mirabilis', and, of course, in 'High Windows'.

SOLITUDE AND SOCIETY

On a personal level, Larkin was a man who liked his own company, yet had important friendships and could be sociable at times. Many of the poems in *High Windows* explore the relationship between the individual and society, some focusing on solitude, others commenting on the value of community and social responsibility.

CONTEXT

Sir John Weston, former British Ambassador to the United Nations and NATO, penned a pastiche of 'Homage to a Government' to comment on Britain's role in Iraq (*Independent on Sunday*, 29 September 2002) beginning with the lines: 'Next year we are to send the soldiers off/ With moral fervour, and this is all right.'

 CHECK THE NET

Go to **www.en.wikipedia. org** for notes on the comedy *No Sex Please, We're British* (1971), which ran in the West End for nearly ten years.

SOLITUDE AND SOCIETY continued

CHECK THE BOOK

Thomas Hardy was another man who valued his solitude and could be said to have felt ambivalent about social contact. However, he wrote warm and affectionate descriptions of communal life, especially at the lower end of the social spectrum, in such novels as *Far from the Madding Crowd* (1874) and *The Mayor of Casterbridge* (1886).

CHECK THE BOOK

Larkin's poem 'Mr Bleaney' in *The Whitsun Weddings* is another poem about loneliness which relates to both 'Friday Night in the Royal Station Hotel' and 'Livings I'. Its **narrator** describes the previous occupant of his shabby boarding house room (in which he uses the same ashtray).

Others explore the pull which Larkin felt between a desire for solitude and the need for company. The poem which demonstrates this in its most extreme form is 'Vers de Société'. Here the people whom the narrator might meet at a social event are summed up as 'a crowd of craps' (1). The time spent with them is:

> time that has flown
> Straight into nothingness by being filled
> With forks and faces. (12–14)

The conversation on offer is 'drivel' (10), whereas time spent 'Under a lamp' alone enjoying the life of the mind is time 'repaid' (14–15). This attitude is echoed in 'Livings II', in which the lighthouse keeper seems to rejoice in his solitude. The sardonic tone of 'Vers de Société' is echoed in 'Sympathy in White Major', in which the imagined posthumous praise of those with whom the poet has socialised in his lifetime is full of **ironic cliché**. However, 'Vers de Société' also expresses Larkin's intense ambivalence in relation to solitude and society. He admits to wanting people to be 'nice' to him (22) but cannot decide whether it is worth the effort to reciprocate. In the end, he seems to need human company largely to stave off discomfiting thoughts of mortality.

Simple loneliness is another aspect of this theme. 'Livings III' contrasts with 'Livings II' in that the former presents a model of social intercourse which is lively but shallow. In this respect it has something in common with 'The Card-Players', in which the concluding phrase 'The secret, bestial peace!' (14) expresses envy, fascination and disgust in relation to social intimacy. 'Livings I', on the other hand, portrays a man whose life is bleakly lonely. Significantly, he is pictured in a hotel. The hotel in 'Friday Night in the Royal Station Hotel' is a larger and grander one, but it still has a certain shabbiness about it (shown by its unmatching chairs and full ashtrays) which underlines the intense atmosphere of loneliness, isolation and abandonment. A different kind of loneliness is shown in 'The Old Fools'. Here the residents, like the salesman in 'Livings I', are no longer in their own homes, and are alone in a communal setting. They are locked into private memories. The phrase 'some lonely/ Rain-ceased midsummer evening' (33–4) poignantly captures their mood.

An aspect of this sense of isolation and loneliness is being away from home – and therefore not belonging. Both 'Livings I' and 'Friday Night in the Royal Station Hotel' are set in hotels, the residents in 'The Old Fools' are in a nursing home, while the patients in 'The Building' are:

> caught
> On ground curiously neutral, homes and names
> Suddenly in abeyance. (17–19)

At the other end of the spectrum are the poems in which Larkin celebrates a sense of community. The foremost of these is 'Show Saturday', which also manages to connect the twin polarities of social and private worlds. Here, community is seen as a wholly positive thing, even though the poet seems to be outside it, as a detached observer. This detachment, too, is also present in 'Dublinesque', although an element of the personal is introduced in the uncertain naming of 'Kitty, or Katy' (22). There is a more pronounced sense of intimate community in 'The Explosion', in which the doomed miners seem to have known each other from an early age.

Perhaps Larkin best manages to resolve the dichotomy of solitude and society in those poems in which he is present and theoretically a member of the community, and yet sufficiently detached to remain an individual, not obliged to engage in social intercourse. This is true of 'Show Saturday', but even more so of 'To the Sea', where the conventions of English seaside behaviour make it possible to be part of this very loosely-knit community without having to communicate with anyone. Interestingly, Larkin's childhood memory is of being happy at being on his own, still part of the seaside community, and knowing that his parents were nearby, yet left to his own devices.

LOVE, SEX AND RELATIONSHIPS

It is now known that Larkin was not quite the sexual recluse that he was once thought to be, and that he did in fact have relationships with several women during his life (including one or two overlapping ones – see **Historical background: Philip Larkin's life and work**). However, he did have major psychological issues

CHECK THE NET
Larkin has been dubbed 'the hermit of Hull'. See **www.hermitary.com** for 'resources and reflections on hermits and solitude'.

CHECK THE BOOK

The novelist and poet who perhaps wrote more about sex and love than anyone else in the twentieth century was D. H. Lawrence. See, for example, *Sons and Lovers* (1913) and *Women in Love* (1920).

CONTEXT

Russian novelist Leo Tolstoy (1828–1910) is another author who recommended remaining childless. He considered that it would be better for humanity to become extinct.

CHECK THE BOOK

Another poet who wrote ironically about relationships was W. H. Auden. His ballad 'As I Walked Out One Evening' (*Selected Poems*, Faber, 1968) has a lover singing idealistically about his love, only to be interrupted by 'all the clocks in the city', which warn him of the ravages of time.

with sexuality and relationships, and especially with commitment. He alludes to these issues – albeit ascribing them to humanity as a whole – in 'This Be The Verse'. He was certainly very awkward with women as an undergraduate at Oxford and envied Kingsley Amis' ease with them. There are no love poems in *High Windows*, not even retrospective ones like 'Wild Oats' in *The Whitsun Weddings*. The nearest we get to a love poem is 'Forget What Did', and we know only from the biographical information that this is about Larkin stopping his diary because he could not bear to record the pain he experienced when Maeve Brennan began seeing another man (even though Larkin was in a relationship with Monica Jones). (However, 'Show Saturday' could in a sense be dedicated to Monica.)

We see marriage, as an aspect of community, in a positive way, in 'The Explosion', in which wives 'see' their husbands after they have died in an explosion, perhaps a testament to their love. Family life is presented as being harmless, and even a positive part of social ritual, in 'To the Sea'. On the other hand, 'Posterity' reminds us of the curtailment of freedom brought about by marriage, and especially by having children. The failure of many marriages is also alluded to in 'Money'. Another negative image of family life appears in 'Going, Going' – 'Their kids are screaming for more' (21) while the final line of 'This Be The Verse' advises the reader '. . . don't have any kids yourself'.

We also see sexual desire, presented as something harmless and natural, in 'How Distant', in which the sight of a young woman doing her laundry on board ship inspires a young man to sexual fantasies. However, in the other poems in which love, sex and relationships play a part, they do so in an **ironic** and rather jaundiced way. In 'The Card-Players' a drunk 'croaks scraps of songs . . . about love' (8). In 'Annus Mirabilis', a **narrator** who has missed out on sex by being born just too early ironically describes the new era of sexual liberation which supposedly replaced the old sense of shame. We are not supposed to be convinced, any more than we are by the ironic assertions made in 'High Windows'. Here, sexual freedom is described in deliberately crass terms which underline the fact that it has not brought about the promised paradise: human misery is too deeply ingrained.

CONSUMERISM AND MATERIALISM

Through the involvement of money, to some degree at least, in so many of these poems, Larkin recognises the all-pervading role it plays in modern life, both on an individual and national level. There are several poems in *High Windows* which explore the theme of consumerism and materialism, in particular 'Livings', 'Going, Going', 'Homage to a Government' and 'Money'. In others, such as 'Posterity' and '*Vers de Société*', it plays a secondary role.

The narrator of 'Livings I' is not portrayed as greedy, but he is constrained by economic necessity, particularly since the Depression forms a backdrop to the poem and especially to the conversation of the men in the Smoke Room. The hotel owner saves money by using ex-Army sheets. There is even a hint of money in the image of the sky draining down the estuary like the bed of a gold river, as if the nation's money is draining away, overseen by the Customs House. The lighthouse keeper of 'Livings II' is uninterested in money, but the dons or clerics in 'Livings III' discuss the career prospects of a colleague as well as the sale of property. Their material comfort is contrasted with that of their butler Starveling (if we are to read anything into the name), and even more so with the sizar (a poor student) in the final stanza.

'Going, Going' more obviously relates to consumerism and materialistic greed, which are seen as the main threats to the England which Larkin knows and loves. He blames the working classes, as well as the greedy and self-satisfied businessmen whose '. . . spectacled grins approve/ Some takeover bid that entails/ Five per cent profit' but dumps ten per cent more pollution into the estuaries (25–8). However, his concern is that the whole of England will become the first slum of Europe, not that there will be a widening gap between the rich and poor. He may be anti-consumerist but he is certainly not a socialist (see **Background: social and historical background**).

'Homage to a Government' purports to be a political poem, but it is more successful as an anti-materialistic one. Its main theme is that the government is going to bring troops home 'For lack of money' (2). Larkin adds, 'We want the money for ourselves at

CHECK THE BOOK

Another poem by Larkin with an anti-consumerism theme is 'Essential Beauty' in *The Whitsun Weddings*.

CHECK THE NET

See www.en. wikipedia.org for more information on high-rise flats, which were first built in Britain after the Second World War in response to an urgent need for cheap housing to replace slums. They were popular at first, but became associated with crime and social alienation. Type 'Tower blocks' into the search box.

CONSUMERISM AND MATERIALISM continued

home/ Instead of working. And this is all right' (5–6). This appears to be a bitter indictment of British materialism, and even laziness. It is as if British people are going to abandon their colonial responsibility to the rest of the world in order to give up work. The deliberately flat tone of Larkin's language emphasises the **irony** effectively. However, it is a false argument to suggest, as this poem does, that Britain is withdrawing from the international stage simply so that its population can give up work, or that there is something intrinsically shameful in bringing home the troops.

Naturally, the poem, which most explicitly addresses the theme of materialism is 'Money'. In this poem, Larkin presents himself as somebody who is baffled by how others spend their money, and who, hermit-like, has no need for it. The power of money is expressed in the way he **personifies** it. It actually speaks to him, reproaching him and asking him why he does nothing with it when he could use it to go out and buy goods and sex. Larkin appears to be unimpressed with what others do with their money, and comments disparagingly on the fact that you cannot take it with you when you die. The final **stanza** is grimly beautiful. Money is now not just speaking, but singing. Its Siren song offers a promise which is ultimately unfulfilled. The fact that the world can in the end only offer empty material comfort is what Larkin finds 'intensely sad' (16). This vision, looking down on the material world, is in contrast to the more ethereal world glimpsed at the end of 'High Windows'.

The theme of materialism is found to a lesser extent in 'Posterity', in which Jake Balokowsky is, like Larkin himself, obliged to work at something he would rather not be doing, just to sustain himself materially. In 'Vers de Société', too, money could be a factor in the poet's attitude towards social events which he is obliged to attend to some extent for professional reasons. Money enters into 'Show Saturday', in the form of the rather ridiculous pound note man, and in the jobs to which the show-goers must return.

CONTEXT

One of the most outspoken opponents of global capitalism is the film director and author Michael Moore. He particularly criticises what he sees as the exploitation of Third World 'sweatshop' workers by large corporations.

LANGUAGE AND STYLE

VOICES

One of the most pronounced features of Larkin's language is his highly evocative use of a wide variety of tones. One broad distinction which a number of commentators, including Andrew Motion, have noted is that between the demotic – the **vernacular** – and the lyrical, or even the sublime. At one end of the scale there is language which is deliberately vulgar and rather shocking, especially for the 1970s. The outstanding examples are 'This Be The Verse', where the effect is exaggerated by the glib rhythm and transparent rhyme scheme, and 'High Windows', where the use of the vernacular expresses an **ironically** casual attitude to sex. 'The Card-Players', too, uses vernacular verbs ('pisses', 'belching', 'snores', 'farts', 'Gobs') to express the physicality of these low-class drinkers. The drinkers in 'Livings III' are higher up the social scale, but their conversation cannot be called refined.

In these three poems, however, Larkin uses a characteristic technique of juxtaposition, moving swiftly from the demotic to the lyrical or sublime. 'The Card-Players' surprises us with an exultant final line which acknowledges the animal nature of the men, while hinting at something mystical in their intimacy: 'The secret, bestial peace!' (14). 'Livings III' ends by directing our gaze upwards to the Chaldean constellations sparkling in the night sky. This technique is also used in the poem 'Sad Steps', which begins with the poet 'Groping back to bed after a piss' (1) and ends with a reflection on the nature of lost youth. The most remarkable example, however, is found in 'High Windows', where the demotic gives way to a vision of the infinite glimpsed through 'sun-comprehending glass' (18).

> **CONTEXT**
>
> Larkin's phrase 'sun-comprehending glass' can be compared to Shelley's 'Dome of many-colour'd glass' in *'Adonais'* (line 463), which Shelley wrote as a requiem to Keats in 1821.

Larkin's vernacular tone is not always vulgar: sometimes it is merely conversational and **colloquial**. This is most obviously the case where he is echoing the casual speech of adopted **personae**, for example in the italic section of 'High Windows', in Jake Balokowsky's crassly contemptuous conversation in 'Posterity', and in the italic section of 'Sympathy in White Major'. Here the vernacular is used ironically to denote a lack of genuine feeling. In 'Going, Going', Larkin addresses us, perhaps simply as himself, in the vernacular: 'Chuck filth' (16) and 'before I snuff it' (38). This could be seen as an attempt to gain our sympathy for his arguments.

Often, Larkin adopts a flat, neutral tone, so that although the words are well chosen, the verse may seem prosaic on a first reading. As with his use of the demotic, this is sometimes because he has adopted a **persona**. When the agricultural salesman in 'Livings I' speaks to us, the plainness of his language reflects his life. His opening line could hardly be more prosaic. This tone is used in a more loaded way in 'Homage to a Government', where it reflects **ironically** the ordinariness of an imagined speaker and the drabness of a life in which money is more important than national pride or virtue. In 'The Building', the matter-of-fact tone of some lines helps to create a sense of unease and foreboding.

In 'Show Saturday' an occasionally neutral tone reflects detached observation on the part of the poet. When, for example he describes the wrestling, he could almost be a visitor from another planet, uncomprehendingly recording what he sees. However, this poem is characterised elsewhere by the affectionately amused tone used to describe the characters ('Children all saddle-swank', 'husbands on leave from the garden/ Watchful as weasels' [50–2]) and an appreciative tone ('all worthy, all well done', [33]). Several other poems contain elements of humour, for example, 'The Card-Players' and 'This Be The Verse', but often of an ironic nature. 'To the Sea' is not humorous, but it shares with 'Show Saturday' a certain warmth and affection.

CHECK THE BOOK

A poem which refers to the moon in a lyrical and romantic way is Ted Hughes' 'Song', which begins, 'O lady, when the tipped cup of the moon blessed you . . .' (*Selected Poems*, Faber, 1962).

Irony, in fact, is a particular feature of *High Windows*. There is the wicked irony of '*Vers de Société*', which begins by **satirising** an invitation: '*My wife and I have asked a crowd of craps/ To come and waste their time and ours*' (1). This inflates a balloon of pretence which is burst by the delightfully gruff response '*In a pig's arse, friend*' (3). The final stanza of 'Sympathy in White Major' is similarly ironic, though less bitingly so. Larkin turns the ironic tone on himself in 'Sad Steps', mocking his own talent for lyricism: '*Lozenge of love! Medallion of art!*' (11). This line is also an example of an exclamatory tone which Larkin occasionally uses, for example in the final line of 'The Card-Players' and in 'Livings II'.

Another tone present in a number of poems – and more so in this collection than in previous ones – is anger. Larkin can be angry on a personal level, as in 'Vers de Société', which is scathing in its dismissal of empty socialising, or he can be angry about developments in society, as in 'Going, Going' and 'Homage to a Government'. The latter contains a quiet, contained anger in its ironic platitudes. In 'The Old Fools', Larkin expresses his anger more forcefully – at the 'whole hideous inverted childhood' (47) of old age.

At other times, Larkin's tone can be yearning, as in 'How Distant', 'Cut Grass' and 'The Trees', or mournful as in 'Forget What Did'. The way in which 'Friday Night in the Royal Station Hotel' evokes loneliness and isolation has something in common with 'The Building'. 'The Explosion' and 'Dublinesque' both involve death and are unusually tender in tone, with no trace of irony.

FICTIONAL ELEMENTS

Some of the poems in the collection contain elements that one might associate with fiction: **narrative**, characterisation and setting. Several, including 'To the Sea', 'Show Saturday' and 'The Explosion', contain a narrative element. Others, such as 'The Building' and 'Dublinesque', describe a scene in which people play a major part. In a third category of poems, Larkin either speaks directly to us or adopts a persona. In 'Posterity', for example, Larkin presents the sharply caricatured Jake Balokowsky, and much of the poem is in speech marks, in his voice, with an appropriate use of the **vernacular**. 'Livings I' uses the persona of the salesman more subtly, even giving it some development when, in a moment of lyricism, he looks at the view from his window. 'Livings II' adopts the enigmatically poetic persona of the lighthouse keeper, and 'Livings III' that of a rather worldly don. Other poems briefly adopt an anonymous persona, as in 'High Windows', with the italicised voice of the older generation: *'That'll be the life . . .'* (11).

CHECK THE BOOK

A modern poem which adopts an effective persona is 'Education for Leisure', by Carol Ann Duffy (from *Standing Female Nude*, Anvill Press, 1985). Look too at Robert Browning's 'My Last Duchess' (1842) for an earlier example. It first appeared in his collection *Dramatic Lyrics*.

At other times Larkin portrays characters from the outside, in the 'omniscient author' narrative mode, without adopting a persona. The outstanding example of this is 'The Card-Players', but there are touches of it towards the end of 'Show Saturday', for example in the description of the husbands. There is also just enough character portrayal in 'The Explosion' to make us empathise with the doomed miners.

The third 'fictional' element, setting, plays a major part in creating the mood of several poems in the collection. The prime example is 'Friday Night in the Royal Station Hotel', which is entirely about the loneliness of the atmosphere built up by the precisely delineated setting. 'The Building' has much in common with this. There the setting is a backdrop to the human sufferers, but the hospital has a sinister life of its own, with its threatening creepers and 'frightening smell' (7). Setting is also vital in 'The Card-Players', since the inn, with its fire and supplies of ham, is a womb-like haven from the stormy weather outside, and from the outside world as a whole.

CHECK THE BOOK

An author whose settings are particularly atmospheric is Dickens. See, for example, the opening to *Bleak House* (1852–3), which describes London in a thick fog.

In 'Show Saturday' and 'To the Sea' the settings are even more important. In the former, the setting is really the show itself, although we do glimpse the surroundings. In the latter, the seaside is an evocative backdrop to social ritual. In 'Cut Grass', the setting is rural England and the feelings evoked by its leafy lanes are all-important. In other poems, there is no single setting, but places are glimpsed, as in 'How Distant', which takes us from the 'married villages' (7) to the huge promise of the ship bound for Australia.

PRECISION AND UNCERTAINTY

Many of the poems in *High Windows* are very closely observed. The supreme example of this is 'Show Saturday', in the detailed description of the entries for the village produce competition. Detail is used to create intense atmosphere in 'Friday Night in the Royal Station Hotel': 'Clusters of lights over empty chairs/ That face each other, coloured differently' (2–3). 'The Building' also employs a lot of detail, again creating atmosphere. We see the scruffy porters, and 'those who tamely sit/ On rows of steel chairs turning the ripped mags' (9–10). Often Larkin moves us with a telling detail, as in the nest of lark's eggs held up and replaced in the grass by a miner in 'The Explosion'.

One aspect of Larkin's precision is his use of hyphenated and compound words to make a description more exact and more compact. For example, in 'Show Saturday' we find 'one-street villages' (44), 'dog-breeding wool-defined women' (4) and 'car-tuning curt-haired sons' (5). 'This Be The Verse' uses the **oxymoronic** 'soppy-stern' (7) to describe the older generation. Other poems use hyphenated words to describe aspects of nature; for example, 'wind-picked' ('Sad Steps', [5]) and 'air-sharpened' ('*Vers de Société*', [17]). Other examples are found in 'Livings II' and 'The Old Fools'.

At other times Larkin's choice of words can be tentative, expressing an uncertainty or ambivalence, sometimes using parenthesis:

> The headed paper, made for writing home
> (If home existed)
>
>   ('Friday Night in the Royal Station Hotel', [12–13])

The effect is to create an unsettling atmosphere in which nothing can quite be relied on. Similar examples are found in 'Annus Mirabilis' and '*Vers de Société*'.

SYMBOLISM AND IMAGERY

Larkin uses a variety of symbols and **imagery**. Some poems are almost devoid of imagery, like 'Posterity' and 'Homage to a Government', while a few others, like 'Livings II' are rich in imagery. Others contain just one or two telling images, like 'This Be The Verse', in which misery is memorably seen as deepening 'like a coastal shelf' (10).

Some of the poems are notably **symbolist** in approach – leading some critics to suggest that Larkin was more influenced than he admitted by French **Symbolist** poets like Baudelaire and Mallarmé (see **Background: Literary background**). The poems that stand out as symbolist in character are: 'The Trees', 'High Windows', 'Sad Steps', 'Solar', 'Money' and 'Cut Grass'. In these poems, a central object carries a burden of symbolic weight. In 'The Trees', it is, of course, the trees themselves, which symbolise a hope for renewal (albeit a rather forlorn hope). In 'Cut Grass', the grass itself is a symbol of the frailty of human life. In 'Sad Steps', Larkin presents the moon as a symbol of romantic aspirations and of youth. In

CHECK THE BOOK

For an example of the poetry of Baudelaire, see *Les Fleurs Du Mal* (Dover Publications, 1992 – in French and English).

'Solar', perhaps the most perfectly symbolist poem in *High Windows*, the sun embodies the generosity of the universe, remote, self-contained, yet giving of itself 'for ever' (18). In 'High Windows', the evocative **symbolism** comes at the end, in the windows and the blue sky seen through them. 'Money' is a sort of negative version of 'High Windows', in that it culminates in a vision not of the infinite, but of material limitation.

WINDOWS

Windows are, appropriately, the most frequently occurring **motif** in the collection, though they are used, symbolically, in a variety of ways. The visions at the end of 'High Windows' and 'Money' are seen through windows. Here the windows are both a medium through which the vision is revealed, 'sun-comprehending' ('High Windows', [18]), and a barrier between the individual and the world, or between the individual and the infinite. They separate internal and external worlds. The window performs a similar function in 'Sad Steps', in which the narrator parts his bedroom curtains to see the moon through his window, which inspires the rest of the poem. The lyrical vision of the estuary in 'Livings I' is presumably viewed through the salesman's hotel window. In 'How Distant' the 'random windows' at the end of the poem seem to offer a magical hope for the future.

In some poems, however, windows are a barrier. The elderly in 'The Old Fools' can only look out at 'The blown bush at the window' (32), unable to return to the outside world. In 'The Building', the windows evoke longing, as the waiting patients look through them at the outside world of everyday normality, a world which some of them may never rejoin. In 'Forget What Did' the 'windows/ Of an opaque childhood' (11–12) blot out what the diarist is unable, or does not wish, to remember.

LIGHT AND DARK

Larkin uses light and dark in a variety of ways. It is certainly not possible to say that light is good and dark bad. Sometimes, as in poems like 'Friday Night in the Royal Station Hotel' and 'Dublinesque', it is not even possible to say that light is light! One outstanding use of light as a symbol is found in 'Livings II', in

> **CONTEXT**
>
> Shakespeare's *Macbeth* contains a great deal of **imagery** relating to light and dark, mostly representing good and evil, but also the spark of life, as in 'Out, out, brief candle' (V.5.23).

which the **narrator** is a lighthouse keeper. The beam of his lighthouse protects his solitude, keeping the outside world at bay by warning it to keep its distance. This can be compared with the narrator's lamp in 'Vers de Société'. In both, light seems to be a symbol of inner light, inspiration and the private intellect.

In 'Livings III' and 'The Card-Players', candlelight and firelight symbolise comfort, the spark of life. The gas fire in 'Vers de Société' is a solitary version of this. Often, however, light is threatening. In 'The Building', the hospital is a honeycomb of light in which individuality is lost, and in which the glare of reality is unavoidable. In 'Friday Night in the Royal Station Hotel' the light, disturbingly, 'spreads darkly downwards' (1) and illuminates empty corridors, adding to a sense of isolation. In 'The Old Fools', the 'lighted rooms' (25) inside the old people's heads are pathetic rather than comforting. In 'Dublinesque', 'light is pewter' (2) – that is, leaden.

Often light is seen in contrast to darkness. In 'The Card-Players', the interior light contrasts with the comfortless dark outside. In 'Vers de Société', the trees are 'darkly swayed' (5). In 'Livings II' the lighthouse keeper looks out on a 'Leather-black' sea (25). In 'Sad Steps' the gardens are 'wedge-shadowed' (4) beneath the moon's cold stare. Other examples are found in 'Livings III' and 'The Building'.

NATURE

The natural world is used symbolically in a number of poems. 'The Trees', 'Cut Grass', 'Solar' and 'Sad Steps' have already been discussed. 'The Explosion', though not primarily a symbolist poem, uses the chasing of rabbits and the lark's nest to suggest innocence. The sea is used symbolically in 'To the Sea', 'Livings II' and 'How Distant'. Larkin uses it to represent the enduring nature of social ritual in 'To the Sea', and opportunity in 'How Distant'. In 'Going, Going', Larkin writes about the sea literally, as an example of the natural world becoming polluted by material greed. His regret is sharpened by the fact that if even this symbol of endurance and hope can be ruined, there is not much hope for England. In 'Livings II', the symbolism is more **ambiguous**. The sea is a source of huge energy but it also contains an element of threat. Hence it 'explodes upwards' and 'slavers' like a hungry dog (2–3).

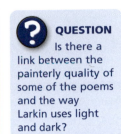

QUESTION
Is there a link between the painterly quality of some of the poems and the way Larkin uses light and dark?

CHECK THE BOOK
There is a great tradition of English nature poetry. One poet whose uncontrived style Larkin might have admired is John Clare. See for example his *Selected Poems* (Everyman Poetry, 2004).

Nature is used in **imagery**, too. The hospital in 'The Building' is a 'clean-sliced cliff' (60); in 'This Be The Verse', misery 'deepens like a coastal shelf' (10); in 'The Old Fools', death is 'Extinction's alp' (41). In 'Solar', the sun (itself a natural symbol) is a 'stalkless flower' (6), and in 'The Old Fools', life is a 'million-petalled flower' (18), suggesting life's infinite variety and opportunity.

Clouds occur in several poems. In 'Sad Steps', they blow apart 'Loosely as cannon-smoke' (8), which may indicate conflict and dissolution, but which could also indicate the dissipation of trouble. In 'Show Saturday', the greyness of the day is not a threat, but in 'To the Sea' and 'Solar', the cloudlessness of the sky more conventionally tokens freedom from trouble.

Wind also features **ambiguously** in some poems. In 'Sad Steps' its restless power blows the clouds apart, and in 'The Card-Players' and '*Vers de Société*', it represents the threat of the outside world. Conversely, in 'Livings II' it helps to protect the **narrator** from the outside world.

RELIGION

CHECK THE BOOK

For more on atheism and the secular society, see Sam Harris, *The End of Faith: Religion, Terror, and the Future of Reason* (Free Press, 2006).

For an avowed atheist, Larkin uses religious imagery surprisingly often. In 'To the Sea', the visit to the seaside is 'half a rite' (18); in 'Show Saturday', the leeks are like 'church candles' (27). In 'Going, Going', the 'carved choirs' (46) are a symbol of religion as an institution – part of old England. In '*Vers de Société*', the hermit is a defunct symbol of religion (and isolation). In the same poem church-going is seen as 'Playing at goodness' (25). In 'Solar', human needs are 'like angels' (19).

However, religion appears most tellingly in 'The Building', where the hospital replaces the cathedral, and where the locked church is a symbol of God being dead. Moreover, the patients have come to 'confess' (22), and their relatives bring 'weak, propitiatory flowers' (64), an indication that in Larkin's world, even if religion is dead, the religious impulse survives.

MONEY

Money is an obvious symbol of materialism in 'Money', but it is more positive in 'Solar', where the sun's 'Gold' is 'Coined . . . among/ Lonely horizontals' (14–15). Similarly, the dead men in 'The Explosion' are seen as 'Gold as on a coin' (23). In 'The Building', money represents the unavoidability of death: 'the only coin/ This place accepts' (56–7). In 'Annus Mirabilis', sexual liberation is 'a brilliant breaking of the bank' (14). The mock exuberance of the **alliteration** emphasises the **irony**.

DISINTEGRATION

There are occasional images of disintegration, as in the view of death in 'The Old Fools': 'the bits that were you/ Start speeding away from each other' (13–14). There is also disintegration in 'Sad Steps', in the separation of the clouds. Closely linked is the image of the sea exploding upwards in 'Livings II'. In 'The Explosion', Larkin delicately implies the physical disintegration of the dead miners in the explosion by contrasting it with 'the eggs unbroken' in the final line.

ISOLATION

It has already been seen that the lighthouse in 'Livings II' is a symbol of isolation. The receding rooms in 'The Building' suggest an individual isolation leading to death. Images suggesting isolation are found in 'The Trees', which, strangely, are seen as 'unresting castles' (9), and 'Friday Night in the Royal Station Hotel', where the hotel is like a fort.

CLOTHING

Clothing appears occasionally in *High Windows*, both **symbolically** and in imagery. At times, clothing is used to indicate character or mood, as in the older generation's old-fashioned hats and coats in 'This Be The Verse', or the doomed patient's washed-out hospital clothes in 'The Building'. Similarly, Jake Balokowsky in 'Posterity' is caricatured as wearing jeans and sneakers, while in 'Show Saturday' the character of the show itself is indicated by the absurd yet charming outfits of the wrestlers. The streetwalkers in 'Dublinesque' show their respect for the deceased, and their

CHECK THE NET

For information and an enlargeable illustration of leg-of-mutton sleeves, go to **www.fashion-era.com**. Click on the link to the 'La Belle Epoque' era to see the paragraph on leg-of-mutton sleeves.

CHECK THE BOOK

In *Macbeth* Shakespeare uses a clothing image when Angus says of Macbeth: 'Now does he feel his title/ hang upon him, like a giant's robe upon a dwarfish thief' (V.2.20–2).

CHECK THE BOOK

Gerard Manley Hopkins uses trees in a similar way to Larkin in his poem 'Spring and Fall', except that for Hopkins it is the trees' loss of leaves that signifies the transitory nature of things: 'Márgarét, áre you gríeving/ Over Goldengrove unleaving?' See *Gerard Manley Hopkins: Selected Poetry* (Oxford World Classics, 1998).

celebration of her life, by their clothing. In 'How Distant', a girl doing her laundry **symbolises** a new start, and the freshness of being young is compared with new shop-bought clothes.

An image which uses clothing in a way which is reminiscent of Shakespeare is found in 'Sympathy in White Major':

> While other people wore like clothes
> The human beings in their days. (9–10)

Here, clothing is a symbol of pretence. The 'other people' have taken up and befriended individuals for their own advantage, to shed them as easily as clothes when it suits them.

PERSONIFICATION

Larkin uses a mixture of **similes** and **metaphors**, but often employs **personification** to bring a concept or something inanimate vividly to life. 'Money' is a fine example of this: money speaks to the poet reproachfully, and in the final **stanza** actually sings in a way which is 'intensely sad' (16). An extended metaphor is used here, in which the singing is like looking down through long french windows on the depressing scene of an industrial town. Personification is used, too, in 'The Trees', to convey the force of the trees' effect on the poet. They seem to speak to him, urging him in the final line to 'Begin afresh, afresh, afresh'. A more traditional sort of personification is used in 'Show Saturday', in which time is shown as a blacksmith. Here the technique makes time itself seem timeless, yet relentless in its effects.

'Sad Steps', 'Solar' and 'Cut Grass' all use personification symbolically. In 'Sad Steps', the staring moon is associated with youth, while in 'Solar' the benign aspect of nature is symbolised by the sun's leonine face and open-handed generosity. In 'Cut Grass', the dying grass symbolises human mortality and therefore exhales like a living, breathing creature. A related image is found in 'The Building', in which the old 'close-ribbed' streets around the hospital 'rise and fall/ Like a great sigh out of the last century' (3–4).

THE USE OF COLOUR

A feature of Larkin's poems that closely relates to **imagery** is his use of colour. Most notably, white is used to symbolise innocence, as in the children's clothes in 'To the Sea' and the flowers and 'white hours' in 'Cut Grass' (5). In 'The Building', the 'white rows' (54) of patients suggest the antiseptic, depersonalised nature of hospitals. In 'Sympathy in White Major', white seems a positive thing as the colour of the foaming drink, but as an image of *'a decent chap . . . the whitest man I know'* (17–23), it is **ironic**. Larkin may be suggesting that being 'white' is being without true character, or just that no one is really that unblemished. In 'Show Saturday', the blanched leeks, like church candles, suggest purity of purpose. The 'salt-white cordage' (3) in 'How Distant' is similar. Conversely, black, when it appears, is threatening, as in the 'Grape-dark' clouds and 'Leather-black' sea in 'Livings II' (12, 25). Grey is used to denote drabness in 'Going, Going'. However, in 'Dublinesque' it seems to be used, in 'pewter' (2), only to create a slightly sombre mood. At the start of 'Show Saturday' it merely serves to demonstrate the resilience of the show goers, in that they turn out in such numbers on a grey day.

A number of other colours are used symbolically in the collection, the most positive being gold and green. Gold is used as a symbol of beauty, preciousness and wealth in 'Livings I', 'Solar' and 'The Explosion'. Closely related is the yellow sand of 'To the Sea'. Green is used to represent hope and renewal in 'The Trees' and 'How Distant', and, as the colour of grass, to symbolise innocence in 'Cut Grass' and 'The Explosion'.

RHETORICAL DEVICES

Larkin uses a number of **rhetorical devices** in *High Windows*, to achieve various effects, especially persuasion. The most striking of these is **synecdoche**, the naming of a part of something to stand for the whole. Larkin uses it, for example, in *'Vers de Société'*, where 'forks and faces' (14) represent the emptiness of social events. The 'knives and glass' are representative items in 'Friday Night in the Royal Station Hotel', part of the table settings that suggest a 'larger loneliness' (5). A single place setting emphasises the solitude of the lighthouse keeper in 'Livings II'. In 'Going, Going', corporate

CHECK THE BOOK

For the psychology of colour, see *The Beginner's Guide to Colour Psychology* (Colour Affects, 1998).

RHETORICAL DEVICES continued

QUESTION
A feature of *High Windows* is its use of negative language, defining things by what they are not. The prime example is in the title poem, in which the 'deep blue air . . . shows/ Nothing, and is nowhere, and is endless' (20). What others can you find – for example, in 'To the Sea', 'Solar' and 'Friday Night in the Royal Station Hotel'?

QUESTION
Some critics think that the poet Gerard Manley Hopkins overuses alliteration. Do you think Larkin ever does this, for example near the end of 'Show Saturday'?

smugness is represented by 'spectacled grins' (25). Another example is found in 'Annus Mirabilis', where marriage is indicated by the phrase 'a wrangle for a ring' (8).

Larkin uses **rhetorical questions** to express anger and horror in 'The Old Fools': 'Why aren't they screaming?' (12) and 'How can they ignore it?' (24), and in the series of incredulous questions which rise to a climax at the end of the poem.

Larkin also uses **hyperbole** occasionally to express anger or contempt, as in 'half my evenings' and 'the drivel of some bitch/ Who's read nothing but *Which*' ('*Vers de Société*', [8–11]). A different effect is achieved by his use of repetition, used **ironically** in 'Homage to a Government' ('Next year', 'orderly' and 'all right'), to create a sense of pathos in 'Annus Mirabilis', and to emphasise how nothing really changes in 'This Be The Verse'.

Larkin frequently uses the poetic techniques (technically, **rhetorical devices**) of **alliteration** and **assonance**, especially the former. He does this in a number of ways, but generally the words that he alliterates are brought into closer relationship. At times Larkin uses alliteration mockingly or disparagingly. The shallowness of the dons' conversation in 'Livings III' is implied by the alliterated list of their topics: 'rheumy fevers, resurrection,/ Regicide and rabbit pie' (15–16). Here, 'resurrection' and 'Regicide' are also connected by assonance. The point is that the topics are more or less random, connected only by sound. If there a connection in sense between 'resurrection' and 'Regicide', it is a rather sacrilegious one, since resurrection would probably refer to Christ, whereas regicide is the more general and secular crime of king-killing. Alliteration is used in a similar way to equate 'prayers and proofs' (22) in the final stanza.

Alliteration is also used mockingly in 'Sad Steps', in 'Lozenge of love!' (11). In 'The Card-Players', the phrase 'Gobs at the grate' (13) emphasises Jan's coarseness. On the other hand, alliteration and assonance are used in a way which is more affectionate than satirical in 'Show Saturday', for example in 'Children all saddle-swank, mugfaced middleaged wives' (51) The alliterative effect is to persuade us that the poet's analysis is correct, purely because the words connect by sound.

METRE, RHYTHM AND RHYME

Many of the poems in *High Windows* have a fairly strict **metre** and rhyme scheme, but it is evidence of Larkin's skill in making verse sound natural that this is usually not obvious. These structural elements give the poem a satisfying feel, an authority, without being intrusive. This is especially true where the rhyme scheme is fairly complex, as in 'To the Sea', 'Friday Night in the Royal Station Hotel', 'Going, Going' and 'Show Saturday'.

'*Vers de Société*' is a special case. Here, the first and last **stanzas** are in rhyming couplets, but the stanzas in between are rhymed more subtly, each stanza in a slightly different way.

Although the use of rhyme is pleasing in itself, especially when made more subtle by the use of **enjambment** (as in 'To the Sea' or '*Vers de Société*'), Larkin also uses it to bring words into special relationship. For example, in stanza 2 of 'To the Sea', 'white' is rhymed with 'rite'. This makes a connection between the innocence and purity of the children and the idea of a religious rite. Similarly, in the final stanza, Larkin rhymes 'cigars' and 'cars', both being largely male preserves in the era in which Larkin was writing.

Other poems deliberately make the metre and rhyme scheme more obvious. This helps, for example, to make 'This Be The Verse' memorable. Its bouncy **iambic** metre, **end-stopped** lines (with relatively little enjambment) and simple ABAB rhyme scheme give it a tongue-in-cheek vigour. Almost the same can be said for 'Annus Mirabilis', though there the rhyming is more subtle (ABBAB). In the more lyrical poems, such as 'Cut Grass' and 'The Trees', the obvious rhyme schemes have a simple charm. Conversely, the rhyming couplets of 'Money' suggest the drabness of materialism.

Some of the poems have a metre but do not rhyme. This seems appropriate for the respectful tone of 'Dublinesque' and 'Solar'. It also fits the freedom embodied in the lives of the young in 'How Distant', where a slightly dreamlike quality is produced by the short lines, which force a pause, as in 'Rising and falling' (4) and 'Melodeons play' (8).

? QUESTION
Larkin's rhymes are often not obvious. It is quite possible to read some of the poems in *High Windows* for the first time and not notice that they rhyme. How much do you think rhyme adds to a poem if it is not obvious?

PART FOUR

CRITICAL HISTORY

CONTEXT

Richard Murphy called 'Livings' 'a bewildering triptych'. A triptych, strictly speaking, is a collection of three separate but thematically connected paintings, originally in medieval religious art. Triptychs were sometimes displayed on boards joined by hinges. In a sense this is quite an appropriate term to use for 'Livings'.

INITIAL RECEPTION

Larkin had at one time been associated with The Movement (see **Background: Literary background**) whose members rejected obscurity in verse. Moreover, many critics regarded his special forte as the writing of transparent verse in a 'conversational' style. Consequently, some critics initially found *High Windows* obscure and difficult compared with Larkin's previous volumes. Clive James, who reviewed the collection for *Encounter* (June, 1974), was generally approving, but complained that poems like 'Livings' (especially part II) and 'Sympathy in White Major' were obscure and **allusive**. He wrote: 'While wanting to be just the reverse, Larkin can on occasion be a difficult poet.' He later called Larkin 'the poet of the void' (in 'Don Juan in London', in *At the Pillars of Hercules*, p. 61).

Referring to the Clive James review, Richard Murphy wrote in the *New York Review of Books* (May, 1975) about:

> a bewildering triptych called 'Livings', which Clive James has deciphered in a penetrating essay: it juxtaposes three separate lives in far-off periods and places, each full of its own comforting certainties that seem faintly threatened in mysterious ways, the implication being that they are on the verge of catastrophe.

Although one might take issue with this interpretation, the important point here is that the reviewer is using words like 'bewildering', 'deciphered', 'mysterious', 'seem' and 'implication'.

American poet Robert Lowell, to whom Larkin anxiously sent an advance copy of the volume, replied:

> I like the title poem best maybe. All the poetry is in the last lines, these would count for little without the others . . . I think you resemble Graves and maybe Auden at times, but the poet I most think of still is Herbert – elegance and homeliness. (*Required Writing*, Faber, 1983)

CONTEXT

George Herbert (1593–1633) was a devoutly Christian metaphysical poet.

Although Lowell was generally an admirer of Larkin, at a time when Larkin appealed to few Americans, this reply seems to be 'damning with faint praise', although it is interesting that what some critics found obscure in this poem, Lowell liked best.

Early reviews of *High Windows* were, however, mostly positive. Alan Brownjohn, writing in the *New Statesman* (1974) called it a 'profoundly beautiful and remarkable book' and added:

> Despite his disavowal of a poet's obligation to develop, *High Windows* does show an indisputable development in Larkin . . . It's doubtful whether a better book than *High Windows* will come out of the 1970s.

Andrew Motion, summing up the critics' response, writes in *Philip Larkin: A Writer's Life* that they were 'impressed by the book's mixture of impatience and fastidiousness'. The 'impatience', even anger in such poems as 'The Old Fools' and 'Going, Going', is what helped to make the collection's reputation. Contrary to Larkin's own modest assertion that he had 'not developed' as a writer, the critics saw this anger as proving that he had moved on, and could not be dismissed as an elegant elegist for a fading England. This elegance, still present in *High Windows*, as noted by Lowell, was perhaps what made Larkin himself so pleased to be praised by Clive James. Larkin wrote:

> I think it is amazing that such a tough egg as Clive James can find time for my old-maidish reservations, and I was much heartened by the unaffected and generous sympathy of his review. (Letter to Anthony Thwaite, May, 1974)

Some contemporary critics (perhaps Lowell included) objected to the 'bad' or 'foul' language of some of the poems. Larkin responded persuasively, telling John Sparrow, the Warden of All Souls College, Oxford:

> I think it can take different forms. It can be *meant* to be shocking (we live in an odd era when shocking language can be used, yet still shocks – it won't last); it can be funny, in the silly traditional way that such things are funny.

CHECK THE NET

For the life and poems of Robert Lowell, see **www.english.uiuc.edu** and search for the poet.

CHECK THE BOOK

To compare the poems of Larkin and Alan Brownjohn, see the latter's *Collected Poems* (Enitharmon Press, 2006).

CHECK THE NET

For an interesting discussion of Larkin's use of swear words in *High Windows*, see **www.bostonreview.net** and type 'Burt High Windows Larkin' into the search box.

CONTEXT
Gavin Ewart
(1916–95) was a
British poet. Much
of his poetry was
witty and
humorous, for
example his
'Phallus in
Wonderland', and
some of it was
erotic. Larkin
praised him as a
plain-speaking
poet.

CONTEXT
Pieter Brueghel
the Elder
(1525–1569) is the
most famous of a
family of Dutch
painters. He is
known especially
for paintings of
village life
depicting a
colourful variety of
peasant characters
and activities,
often without a
special focus on
any one of them.
In this sense,
'Show Saturday'
does resemble one
of his paintings.

Sales of *High Windows* were, for a book of poetry, very good: 6,000 copies sold within three months, with another 7,500 printed later in the year, and another 6,000 the following January. Larkin had at last become a national institution.

MORE RECENT EVALUATION

Barbara Everett, in an important essay on Larkin (*Essays in criticism*, 30, 1980) develops this investigation of Larkin's **symbolist** tendencies in *High Windows*. Her analysis of 'Sympathy in White Major' is outlined in the commentary on that poem in these Notes. She also comments on 'High Windows' and 'Friday Night in the Royal Station Hotel' in a similar vein.

Terry Whalen, on the other hand, praises Larkin, especially in *High Windows*, for his acute, penetrating powers of observation, and for the way in which his symbolism springs unobtrusively out of this observation of the physical world, so that an observed object, such as the moon in 'Sad Steps', works at the level of simple description. One does not have to apply symbolic interpretation to the object in order to appreciate it at a basic level. Whalen also praises the energy and freshness of Larkin's observation of the physical world:

> It is there, for example, in the virtual tumble of detail from the physical world, which is at the living base of his poem 'Show Saturday'. It is a poem which has a crowded life of its own, a Breughel-like grasp of the immediacy of life's plural detail. ('Philip Larkin's Imagist bias: his poetry of observation' *Critical Quarterly*, Summer 1981)

Whalen goes on to comment on the way in which Larkin's arguments also emerge out of this physical observation, rather than being presented in abstract form. This is the case, for example, in 'The Building', in which we are taken step by step to the conclusion that the hospital is a kind of prison. He particularly praises 'Dublinesque', for its delicate creation of setting and atmosphere from closely observed detail, and for its embodiment of 'a moment of epiphany, one in which the ostensible contradictions in the scene are blended musically into an illumination'.

LARKIN AT SIXTY

Larkin's sixtieth birthday (in 1982, eight years after the publication of *High Windows*) produced a spate of retrospective appraisals, even though he had almost stopped writing poetry by this time. Several of these tributes appeared in *Poetry Review* (82, 2). Gavin Ewart wrote:

> *High Windows* is more regretful in tone [than *The Whitsun Weddings*], but the best poems are equal to his best: 'Livings', 'High Windows', 'The Old Fools', 'Going, Going', 'The Card-Players', 'Posterity', 'This Be The Verse', 'Annus Mirabilis', '*Vers de Société*'. Larkin's books aren't overflowing or technically very exploratory, but they're full of concentrated essences.

Ewart especially praises Larkin in 'Livings III' and 'The Card-Players' for his 'novelistic ability to create a scene with people', and for his talent at finishing a poem, shown especially in 'The Old Fools' and '*Vers de Société*'.

In the same issue, A. N. Wilson admits that Larkin's world is a gloomy one. Nonetheless, he says:

> Reading *High Windows* makes you sorry you barged in; there seem to be 'keep off the grass' notices all over the place and, as with Hardy and Housman, fairly insistent reminders not to make the mistake of thinking the poet is 'nice' or wanting him to be your intimate. Yet . . . it all springs from an absolute certainty of lyric purpose, an unerring touch . . . No poet has ever conveyed the still sad music of humanity in quite Larkin's perfect tone.

Wilson also comments that 'Show Saturday' achieves a 'rather big effect without being remotely grandiose or pompous', and that 'The Trees' 'is one of the most hopeful poems in our language, its beauty springing from the kind of unmannered simplicity which all the best lyrics have had since the Middle Ages'.

CONTEXT

A. N. Wilson (born 1950) is an English novelist, critic and biographer. In 2006 he published a biography of John Betjeman, whom Larkin admired. After publication, he discovered that a letter he had included, sent by 'Eve de Harben' and detailing a previously unknown love affair, was a hoax. 'Eve de Harben' was an anagram of 'Ever Been Had'.

CONTEXT

Seamus Heaney is regarded as one of the foremost poets writing in English today. He was born in 1939 in Londonderry, Northern Ireland. He has published numerous books of poetry, including *North*, published in the year after *High Windows*. He was awarded the Nobel Prize for Literature in 1995.

CONTEXT

Andrew Motion (born 1952) is not only the author of the most highly regarded biography of Larkin, *Philip Larkin: A Writer's Life*, he is also a much-respected poet himself, and is the current Poet Laureate. He is a Professor of Creative Writing at the University of London.

LATER APPRAISALS

Seamus Heaney, in *The Government of the Tongue* (Faber, 1988), comments on the 'Yeatsian need for a flow of sweetness' in *High Windows*, which, he says, 'flows into the poetry most reliably as light'. Heaney particularly singles out 'Sad Steps' and 'Solar'. In the former he admires the way in which Larkin lays bare his temptation to succumb to 'lunar glamour' by romanticising what he sees from his window. In the latter he comments on the phallic nature of the way in which the sun is portrayed, and concludes: 'The poem is unexpected and daring, close to the pulse of primitive poetry, unprotected by any sleight of tone or persona.'

Andrew Motion (in *Philip Larkin*, Methuen, 1982) argues that Larkin is not as pessimistic and curmudgeonly as many people think, and in fact 'his hope of deriving comfort from social and natural rituals is resilient'. He cites, for example, 'The Trees', 'The Explosion' and 'Show Saturday'. However, he acknowledges that Larkin is not a true nature-lover, being more interested in the opportunities nature offers to 'moralise about the human condition'. Motion also highlights an important aspect of Larkin's attitude towards youth and aging – the importance of choice, almost as a defining factor of a life fully lived.

Another feature of *High Windows* on which Motion comments is the great vigour of Larkin's imagination, especially in 'Livings', 'Dublinesque' and 'The Explosion'. While not denying Larkin's much-vaunted talent for describing the material world, he points out the extent to which this collection explores a **symbolist** approach, for example in 'Solar' and 'Money'.

Larkin's attitude towards women and sex has attracted the attention of several critics. Steve Clark, in *Sordid Images: The Poetry of Masculine Desire* (Routledge, 1994) focuses on how Larkin deals with problems of sexual desire and sexual identity. Clark acknowledges Larkin's misogyny but argues that his rejection of sexual norms in poems like 'This Be The Verse' is positive in that it shows how attitudes towards sexual relationships are socially constructed. He writes: 'The sexual politics of Larkin's verse can be seen as one of principled and unillusioned abstention.' In 'Annus

Mirabilis', Clark sees a rejection of the 'homogenisation' of sex, summed up in the line 'Everyone felt the same' (12): Larkin resents being expected to tow the line. Clark astutely points out that *Lady Chatterley's Lover* was a bestseller (largely because of its sexually explicit nature and the controversy which this aroused). The Beatles, too, were hugely popular. Hence both stand for sexuality as perceived in mass culture.

Steve Clark dissents from the general praise of 'High Windows', which he says 'uses a churlish and ungenerous presentation of "everyone young" to support a regression into an ecstatic nullity . . . even if the pursuit of happiness through sexuality is squalid and misguided, that doesn't render religious consolation any the less "outdated".' Unlike many other critics, Clark does not regard the 'symbolist leanings' of *High Windows* as an improvement on Larkin's earlier work.

Clark sees the message of 'This Be The Verse' as specifically masculine, with its rejection of paternity and the line '*Man* hands on misery to *man*' (9). The line 'Get out as early as you can' (11) he sees as referring ultimately to 'the whole cycle of procreation'. In this connection, Clark points out the negative family role assigned to fathers by Larkin. In 'Posterity', for example, it is because of Myra, or at least her 'folks', that Jake Balokowsky has to buckle down to a job he claims he hates. Clark also cites as evidence of Larkin's misogyny the fact that this is one of the few cases where Larkin names a woman in one of his poems. ('Dublinesque' is another, and even there the name is uncertain.)

Janice Rossen, in *Philip Larkin: His Life's Work* ((University of Iowa Press, 1989), puts forward a feminist critique of Larkin. She finds that he falls just short of being a misogynist, and that to call him a misanthropist would be nearer the mark. However, she does note how often women are seen as 'other' in his poems (although they come in for more brutal treatment in poems such as 'Sunny Prestatyn' than in *High Windows*). She comments on his negativity towards women, but considers that this is an expression of his inner conflict between sexual desire and the need to preserve his autonomy – a conflict which Larkin is not the only man to experience. Her analysis of 'High Windows' is that Larkin is

> **CONTEXT**
>
> In a letter to his friend Sutton in 1951, Larkin wrote: 'If I consider my state of permanent non-attachment, my perpetual suspension, my sexual indifferences, I should put it down to Mother-complex if I were honest, I suppose. How irritating! And nasty, too!'

> **CONTEXT**
>
> The US publisher of *High Windows* wanted Larkin to omit 'Posterity' on the grounds that it was anti-semitic, the reference to Tel Aviv and use of the name Myra (a name favoured Jewish Americans) identifying the unlikeable Jake Balokowsky as Jewish. Larkin objected and eventually the poem was included.

CONTEXT

Prestatyn is a North Wales seaside town. Larkin's poem 'Sunny Prestatyn' describes the lewd disfigurement of a poster encouraging people to 'Come to sunny Prestatyn'.

CONTEXT

The British Empire had still been powerful before the Second World War, but in 1946 Britain was exhausted, and the public increasingly saw the Empire as a drain on Britain rather than a resource. There was also a growth of nationalist movements in British colonies. India achieved independence in 1947, and a flood of British colonies separated from Britain over the next two decades. By the publication of *High Windows*, Britain could no longer call itself a significant colonial power.

bemoaning the fact that, despite the sexual revolution, he (or the poem's protagonist) is still so constrained by the old 'shame that started at sixteen' (as he calls it in 'Annus Mirabilis') that he is unable to benefit from it. He is what Jake Balokowsky calls 'One of those old-type *natural* fouled-up guys' (24). However, she also notes the way in which the poem retains a link between sex and money: the revolution is a 'breaking of the bank'. This link is also present in 'Money', where it seems that cash is required to buy pleasure, including sex. (The second wife is mentioned in the same vein as the house and car!) She sees Larkin as essentially conflict-ridden, and taking refuge behind the 'high windows' of detachment. However, she concedes the possibility that he is rejecting the illusions of romantic love rather than women *per se*, and that women bear the brunt of this. The **ironic** exclamations to the moon in 'Sad Steps' bear this out.

Both Stan Smith and Tom Paulin present **historicist** accounts of Larkin. Stan Smith's approach is more Marxist than Paulin's but both see Larkin's poetry as voicing a British response to the nation's post-war decline as a colonial power. Stan Smith's comments on 'Show Saturday' are discussed in the **Extended commentary** on the poem. Paulin (*The Times Literary Supplement*, July, 1990) focuses on Larkin's isolationism as a feature not only of Larkin's psychology but of the British post-war psyche. Of 'Friday Night in the Royal Station Hotel' he comments: 'The poem displaces an English provincial city and makes its author momentarily into an exile.' The hotel is like a colony, a last outpost of British colonialism. A similar, though more exultant, sense of isolation is found in 'Livings II', while the dons in 'Livings III', for Paulin, embody 'a type of desolate selfish comfort which Larkin is torn between hating and hugging'. 'The Card-Players', too, is a poem about protecting oneself from the outside world. Rather unfairly, Paulin cites 'Show Saturday' as an example of an England, created by Larkin, which is cold and joyless, and which is distinctly nationalist. He goes so far as to compare it with the anti-immigration sentiments expressed by Conservative minister Norman Tebbit at the start of his career.

James Booth, on the other hand, in Michael Baron (ed.), *Larkin With Poetry* (English Association, 1997), disputes the ideological interpretations of critics such as Tom Paulin. Booth denies that Larkin's poetry is limited by his attachment to Englishness, and that it is nationalistic. His critique focuses on Larkin's powers as a lyric poet, particularly praising the 'brusque virtuosity' of 'Livings II', and taking issue with Paulin's view that 'Livings' is a poem with a disguised political message.

For more information on the time at which Larkin was writing see **Background: Social and historical background.**

QUESTION
What attitudes towards women do you think Larkin expresses in *High Windows*? See, for example, 'High Windows', 'Dublinesque', 'How Distant', 'Annus Mirabilis' and 'Show Saturday'.

PART FIVE

BACKGROUND

PHILIP LARKIN'S LIFE AND WORK

Philip Larkin was born in Coventry, on 9 August, 1922, the second child and only son of Sydney and Eva Larkin. His sister, Katherine, known as Kitty, was several years older. Larkin later wrote that he saw himself, to all intents and purposes, as an only child. According to his later accounts, Larkin's childhood was not a happy one, although he never suffered material deprivation, and was coddled by his mother. He was a sensitive child, and he developed a stutter from early on which added to his shyness. He did not get on well with other children, and later said that it was a revelation to him when he realised that it was not people he loathed, but children. The stutter, which was only on words beginning with vowels, had largely left him by his mid-thirties.

Larkin's parents were ill-suited to each other and bickered much of the time. His father was a rather remote man who expected his wife to be the home-maker, but nonetheless despised her for it. Kitty later said that he adored Philip, but according to Larkin he rarely showed it. He was an accountant, and was City Treasurer of Coventry from 1922 to 1944. He was also an admirer of Nazism (remaining so even during the war) and in 1937 took the fifteen-year-old Philip on holiday to Germany. Some of this influence imprinted itself on Larkin, who remained right-wing in his politics, and later became a supporter of the Conservative Prime Minister Margaret Thatcher. Even in 1941, when Larkin was a student at Oxford, worrying about being called up, he wrote to his friend Jim Sutton about Hitler's speeches, saying:

> I looked into them and felt the familiar sinking of heart when I saw how *right*, and yet how *wrong* everything had been. The disentanglement of this epoch will be a beautiful job for someone. (Quoted in: Motion, *Philip Larkin: A Writer's Life*, p. 53)

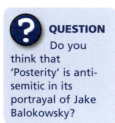

QUESTION
Do you think that 'Posterity' is anti-semitic in its portrayal of Jake Balokowsky?

In 1930, Larkin entered King Henry VIII Grammar School in Coventry. A quiet boy – not least because of his stutter – he attracted little attention from his teachers. By the time he entered his teens he was an avid reader, encouraged by his father's surprisingly liberal taste in literature, and his large library. He also began writing privately, unknown to all but a few of his friends. He had worked on four novels by the time he left school. He had also contributed to the school magazine, which he co-edited in his final year.

In the 1940, Larkin became a student at St John's College, Oxford, studying English Literature. Like his school, this was a single-sex environment. Larkin's writings from this time, including letters to friends, suggest that he spent more time fantasising about women than he spent in their company. He was by all accounts very awkward with the women that he did meet, and he envied Kingsley Amis his relative ease with them.

Larkin found it difficult to settle down to his studies, partly because he expected to be called up for National Service. In 1941 he was immensely relieved to discover that his bad eyesight had caused him to fail his medical examination. Despite this, his writings of the time paint a picture of him spending more time listening to jazz and drinking heavily than studying. Nonetheless, he continued to write, being influenced by Auden, Yeats and Hardy. At this point he saw himself largely as a budding novelist rather than a poet, although he was delighted when he managed to get a poem published in *The Listener* in November 1940. It is from this period that his novel *Trouble at Willow Gables* dates. Set in a girls' boarding school, it is part spoof, part voyeuristic erotica. Its tone suggests that Larkin found sex with real women an exciting but daunting prospect. He even had a brief homosexual encounter with a fellow undergraduate at this time.

Although adopting a rather cavalier attitude towards his studies, as Larkin approached his finals he became very anxious to do well, and feared the worst – perhaps even complete failure. He was therefore extremely pleased, though incredulous, when he received a first-class degree.

CHECK THE NET

Larkin's old school is still a grammar school. Visit its website at **www.kinghenrys. co.uk**. Larkin is mentioned as one of a number of illustrious former students.

CHECK THE BOOK

See *Trouble at Willow Gables and Other Fiction 1943–53* (Faber, 2002).

CHECK THE NET

Find out more about Wellington, where Larkin first worked as a librarian at www. shropshiretourism. info/wellington

On leaving Oxford, Larkin had no particular ambition, other than to be a writer. However, he knew that he had to earn a living somehow. Partly encouraged by his father, he made two unsuccessful attempts to join the civil service before deciding to apply for a job as a librarian. He began work in Wellington, Shropshire, in November 1943. In 1946, he became assistant librarian at University College, Leicester. Despite having an **lukewarm** attitude towards any work other than writing, he took his professional duties seriously, studying for qualifications in his spare time and becoming a member of the Library Association in 1949. He became sub-librarian at Queens University, Belfast, in 1951, and then librarian at the University of Hull in 1955. He remained in this post until 1985, the year in which he died.

Larkin's public **persona** during his lifetime, and at least until the publication of his correspondence in 1992, was of a determined bachelor who had little to do with women, sexually inhibited and morose. His diaries and letters contain numerous assertions that he found women tiresome ('stupid beings') and sex more trouble than it was worth ('always disappointing and often repulsive'). Nonetheless, he had relationships with several women, even if sex continued to be a rather vexed issue for him – as shown by poems like 'Annus Mirabilis' and 'This Be The Verse'. However, the sexually frustrated persona of 'Annus Mirabilis' represents an aspect of his personality rather than the man in his entirety.

 **QUESTION** Larkin's reputation declined, at least for a while, after his private letters showed him to be sexist and mildly racist. Do you think that we should take this into account when assessing the value of his poetry?

Larkin's first love was Ruth Bowman, commemorated in his 1962 poem 'Wild Oats' as one of two girls who 'came in where I worked' (the library). The one who caught his eye was a 'bosomy English rose', Jane Exhall, but Ruth Bowman, the 'friend in specs I could talk to', was the one he 'took out' and even became engaged to. His most enduring relationship was with Monica Jones, but he also had a serious long-term relationship with Maeve Brennan, and an affair with Betty Mackereth, a colleague at the University of Hull Library.

CONTEXT

'Wild Oats' is an **ironic** title (probably intentionally so), since the phrase usually refers to a man's sexual encounters before he is 'tamed' by marriage. Larkin never married.

All the time Larkin was working as a librarian he continued to write poetry. His early poems were published in an anthology, *Poetry from Oxford in Wartime* (1944). His first collection, *North Ship*, was published in 1945. In 1946, he published his first novel,

Jill, set in wartime Oxford. His second novel, *A Girl in Winter* (1947), was more successful, though not enough to establish him as a novelist. A more mature and independent poetic voice is apparent in his next collection of poems, *The Less Deceived* (1955). Several of his poems appear in *New Lines*, an anthology of poetry by The Movement (see **Background: Literary background**), with which he was associated at the time. *The Whitsun Weddings*, which some critics consider to be his finest work, was published in 1964, and finally, *High Windows* in 1974. Before this, in 1970, he published a volume of essays on his great musical passion, *All What Jazz*. He also edited *The Oxford Book of Twentieth-Century English Verse* in 1973. It was partly the prestige that this earned him that encouraged him to approach the publisher Faber with the poems that were to become *High Windows*. He told his editor there, Charles Monteith, that he knew the collection was short, but that he felt he was unable to write many more poems in a short space of time. After problems over the American publisher wanting to omit 'Posterity', a further delay arose when Larkin finished another poem, 'Show Saturday', just as the book was going into proof stage. He particularly wanted it to be included, because he felt that it gave the collection the weight that it otherwise lacked. He then discovered that the rhymes were wrong in **stanza** 3 and told his editor that he would have to rewrite it – which he did.

OTHER WORKS BY PHILIP LARKIN

Larkin's early poetry collections, including *The North Ship* (Fortune Press, 1945) were much influenced by Yeats. This collection contains a fine poem about the necessity to end a relationship: 'Love, we must part now: do not let it be'. His two novels, written at about this time, have never achieved great critical acclaim, and might have been forgotten, were it not for Larkin's fame as a poet. *Jill* (1946) is set in the wartime Oxford that had become familiar to Larkin. It traces the university career of John Kemp, a working-class Lancashire boy who finds himself even more at sea in the elitist world of Oxford college life than did Larkin (a grammar school boy from a middle-class background). 'Jill' is Kemp's fantasy sister. Larkin's second novel, *A Girl in Winter* (1947), describes a single day in the life of librarian Katherine Lind, who works in a dull English provincial town

CHECK THE BOOK
The actor, Tom Courtenay, wrote and performed a play called *Pretending to be Me*, entirely based on Philip Larkin's letters and poems. It was first performed at the Leeds West Yorkshire Playhouse in November 2002.

QUESTION
Do you think Larkin was right to think that 'Show Saturday' was an important poem to include in the collection? What does it add?

(rather like Larkin's). The novel includes a flashback to an adolescent romance.

Larkin's poetic career became more firmly established with the publication of *The Less Deceived* (Marvel) in 1955. This includes one of his most famous poems, 'Toads', with its innovative, conversational style and its challenging of the work ethic. One of the poems in this collection, 'No Road', is a poignant though subdued account of the end of a relationship, which anticipates some of the **symbolist** poems of *High Windows*. 'Church Going' explores some of the social 'Post-Christian era' themes developed in later collections, including *High Windows*. See, for example, 'To the Sea'. Another rather enigmatic poem, 'Going', explores Larkin's increasing preoccupation with mortality.

The Whitsun Weddings (Faber, 1964) includes **satirical** social comment, mixed with suburban settings. It explores themes developed in *High Windows*. For example, the lonely 'Mr Bleaney' is a predecessor of the agricultural salesman in 'Livings I' and 'The Whitsun Weddings' anticipates 'To the Sea' and 'Show Saturday'. 'Sunny Prestatyn', which has been called misogynistic, nonetheless offers a vigorous comment on male attitudes towards women, and women's depiction by the media.

CHECK THE NET

Find out more about Prestatyn at **www.prestatyn. org.uk**

SOCIAL AND HISTORICAL BACKGROUND

Critics differ in their judgement of the extent to which Philip Larkin was influenced by social and historical changes in the society in which he lived. He was famously provincial in outlook, and had no particular desire to travel. He once said that he would not mind going to China, providing he could come back on the same day.

Although *High Windows* was published in 1974, some of its poems were written much earlier ('Solar', for example, was written in 1964), and the whole collection is informed by the 1960s. This was a decade of rapid change in Britain. Pop music, which had begun to emerge in the 1950s, was developing fast. Britain was doing well economically, and young people had more money than ever to spend on new fashions and records. A new generation was growing up for whom the Second World War was history, and for whom even post-war austerity was a dim memory.

Morality, too, was changing. Faith in God had been undermined by the horrors of the war. However, the religious impulse itself had not entirely disappeared, and many of the poems in *High Windows* demonstrate this – notably 'The Building'. The 1960s saw a growth in alternative spirituality amongst young people. Hippies embraced 'flower power'. The Beatles went to India to learn meditation in the ashram of the Maharishi Yogi. Mind-altering drugs were widely available, encouraging people to 'tune in, turn on, and drop out' (in the words of Timothy Leary). The contraceptive pill helped to bring about what was widely called the sexual revolution – alluded to in Larkin's 'Annus Mirabilis'. (Interestingly the 'revolution' did not extend to men having to take prime responsibility for contraception, and in fact it diminished their responsibility somewhat.) There was also widespread suspicion of materialism, especially among young people, some of whom increasingly challenged the establishment and the beginnings of what in our time has come to be called global capitalism.

Although Larkin never came close to tuning in, turning on, or dropping out, he was strongly anti-materialistic, as is shown by 'Going, Going' and 'Money'. He was also aware of the sexual revolution, as shown in 'High Windows' and 'Annus Mirabilis', even if he was sceptical about its real potential for ending human suffering, and even if he felt that he had personally missed out on it.

The 1960s were also a period during which Britain was rapidly declining as a colonial power. Critics such as Tom Paulin have argued that Larkin's poetry, in its conservative, regressive, isolationist tendencies, expresses the mood of the national psyche in the face of this decline. This was also a period of mass immigration from Britain's former colonies, and particularly from India and Pakistan. There was a rise in racism, and right-wing racist politics. Some politicians warned against the dangers of immigration. Enoch Powell, for example, made his famous 'rivers of blood' speech in which he warned of the violence that would ensue if Britain allowed further immigration. It is notable that there is not a single

CHECK THE BOOK
Find out about the 1960s' most famous pop band the Beatles in Chris Ingham's *The Rough Guide to the 'Beatles'* (Rough Guide Music Guides, 2006).

QUESTION
Do you feel that a poet has an obligation to comment on his society? Was Larkin perfectly within his rights to ignore the new immigrant population in his poetic view of England?

black or Asian face in *High Windows*. Although Larkin's does not actually speak up against immigration, the England that he wants to preserve, shown angrily in 'Going, Going' and affectionately in 'Show Saturday', does seem to be a traditional one that harks back to a time before large-scale immigration. It is also known from his private writings that he was at least mildly racist. On the other hand, he was unusually frank in these private writings, and enjoyed shocking people with his lack of political correctness – even before the term had been invented. It also has to be added that he was a great jazz fan and admired many black musicians.

LITERARY BACKGROUND

During his early career, Larkin was influenced by Yeats, Auden, Edward Thomas and Thomas Hardy. Some of his early lyricism, especially, can be traced to Yeats. His embracing of a pastoral Englishness has much in common with Edward Thomas. Thomas Hardy, whom Larkin continued to admire, had a similarly morose outlook on life, but was also capable of a precise observation of the material world – a feature which became a special strength in Larkin's work.

THE MOVEMENT

Larkin is often thought of as having been influenced by a group of British poets, known as 'The Movement'. This group developed its ideas largely by rejecting those of previous poets. T. S. Eliot, Ezra Pound and the Modernists had been almost deliberately obscure, but the Movement embraced clarity. W. H. Auden and other poets of the 1930s had emphasised the poet's social and political role, but the Movement eschewed this. In fact, Larkin never became seriously involved in political debate, either in his personal life or in his poetry. 'Going, Going' and 'Homage to a Government' are probably the nearest he gets, and those contain what is more like knee-jerk reaction than serious political comment.

Other poets thought of as members of the Movement are Robert Conquest, Donald Davie, D. J. Enright, Ted Hughes, George Macbeth, Vernon Scannel and John Wain. However, Larkin rapidly developed a poetic voice that was quite distinct from these poets. Ted

CHECK THE BOOK
For an entertaining but informative illustrated introduction to Modernism, see Chris Rodriques, *Introducing Modernism* (Icon Books, 2004).

CHECK THE BOOK
See D. J. Enright's *Collected Poems 1948–98* (Oxford Poets, 1998).

Hughes, for example, the poet whose stature was equal to that of Larkin, is only superficially similar. He has Larkin's moroseness, but not his sense of humour or irony. They share an interest in describing the real material world in close detail, but their conclusions are different. And whereas Ted Hughes frequently writes about nature, and strives to express its raw power, Larkin is more interested in nature as a symbol, and as an aspect of Englishness.

CHECK THE BOOK

For Ted Hughes, see *Collected Poems of Ted Hughes* (Faber, 2005).

CHECK THE BOOK

See George Macbeth, *Selected Poems*, ed. Anthony Thwaite, with an introduction by Carol Ann Duffy (Enitharmon Press, 2002).

World events	Larkin's life	Literary events
		1917 Edward Thomas dies
	1922 Born in Coventry	**1922** T. S. Eliot, *The Waste Land*
		1927 Virginia Woolf, *To the Lighthouse*
		1928 Death of Thomas Hardy; D. H. Lawrence publishes *Lady Chatterley's Lover*
	1930 Pupil at King Henry VIII School, Coventry	**1930** Hardy's *Collected Poems* published
1932–9 Spanish Civil War **1933** Nazis seize power in Germany		
		1934 Robert Graves, *I, Claudius*; T. S. Eliot, *Murder in the Cathedral*
	1936 Holiday in Germany with father	
	1937 Second holiday in Germany	**1937** George Orwell, *The Road to Wigan Pier*
1939–45 Second World War	**1939** Edits school magazine, *The Coventrian*	**1939** Yeats publishes *Last Poems and Two Plays*, and dies; James Joyce, *Finnegan's Wake*
	1940 Student at Oxford University; befriends Kingsley Amis and Bruce Montgomery; first nationally published poem appears in *The Listener*; Coventry blitzed by German Luftwaffe	
	1943 Fails army medical exam; graduates with first-class honours in English; first job as librarian in Wellington, Shropshire; meets Ruth Bowman	

World events	Larkin's life	Literary events
	1945 Has poems in *Poetry from Oxford in Wartime* and publishes *The North Ship*	**1945** George Orwell, *Animal Farm*
1946 Gandhi assassinated	**1946** Publishes novel, *Jill*; Assistant Librarian, University of Leicester	
	1947 Second novel, *A Girl in Winter*; meets Monica Jones	
	1948 Father dies	
1950 London Dock Strike	**1950** Sub-librarian at Queen's University, Belfast	
	1951 Publishes *XX Poems*	
		1952 Dylan Thomas, *Collected Poems*; Samuel Beckett, *Waiting for Godot*
1954 McCarthy persecuting suspected Communist sympathisers in USA		**1954** Kingsley Amis, *Lucky Jim*; Dylan Thomas, *Under Milk Wood*
	1955 Becomes Librarian at University of Hull (remains there for thirty years); meets Maeve Brennan (later his lover); publishes *The Less Deceived*	**1955** V. Nabokov, *Lolita*; W. H. Auden, *The Shield of Achilles*
1956 Suez Crisis		
		1958 Harold Pinter, *The Birthday Party*; Samuel Beckett, *Krapp's Last Tape*
		1960 *Lady Chatterley's Lover* ban lifted; Kingsley Amis, *Take a Girl Like You*; John Betjeman, *Summoned by Bells*

World events	Larkin's life	Literary events
1961 Eichmann found guilty of war crimes		
1962 Cuban Crisis		
1962 Commonwealth Immigrants Act		
1963 Kennedy assassinated; Profumo scandal; Macmillan resigns; Beatles first LP; the contraceptive pill is introduced in Britain		
1964 Martin Luther King awarded Nobel Peace Prize; Harold Wilson elected Labour Prime Minister	**1964** Publishes *The Whitsun Weddings*	
1965 Race Relations Board set up	**1965** Awarded Queen's Gold Medal for Poetry	
		1966 Seamus Heaney, *Death of a Naturalist*; Tom Stoppard, *Rosencrantz and Guildenstern are Dead*
1967 Homosexual acts between consenting adults legalised in England and Wales; Wilson government announces intention to withdraw British troops from east of Suez		**1967** Ted Hughes, *Wodwo*
1968 Enoch Powell's 'Rivers of blood' immigration speech; British troops leave Aden		
1969 Voting age reduced to eighteen; first Moon landing		**1969** Kingsley Amis, *The Green Man*; John Fowles, *The French Lieutenant's Woman*; W. H. Auden, *City Without Walls*

World events	Larkin's life	Literary events
1970 Edward Heath Conservative Prime Minister	**1970** Publishes *All What Jazz: A Record Diary*	**1970** Ted Hughes, *Crow*
		1971 John Osborne, *West of Suez*
1972 Miners' strike; 'Bloody Sunday', Northern Ireland (soldiers shoot dead thirteen marchers)	**1972** Mother enters nursing home	**1972** Seamus Heaney, *Wintering Out*
1973 Three-day week to save energy	**1973** Edits *Oxford Book of Twentieth Century Verse*	**1973** W. H. Auden dies
1974 Harold Wilson Labour Prime Minister	**1974** Publishes *High Windows*; receives CBE	**1974** Kingsley Amis, *Ending Up*; Doris Lessing, *Memoirs of a Survivor*; Tom Stoppard, *Travesties*
1975 Margaret Thatcher Leader of Conservative Party		**1975** Seamus Heaney, *North*
1976 Harold Wilson resigns; replaced by James Callaghan		
	1977 Mother dies; chairs Booker Prize panel; last published poem, 'Aubade', in *The Times Literary Supplement*	
1978 World's first test-tube baby born	**1978** Made Companion of Honour	
		1979 Ted Hughes, *Moortown*
1981 Racial tension leads to rioting in Brixton and elsewhere in Britain		
1982 Recession; high unemployment		
	1983 Publishes *Required Writings: Miscellaneous Pieces 1955–82*	
1984 Year-long Miners' Strike begins	**1984** Receives honorary D.Litt. from Oxford University	
	1985 Dies from cancer, aged sixty-three	

OTHER WORKS BY PHILIP LARKIN

The North Ship, Fortune Press, 1945

Jill, Fortune Press, 1946

A Girl in Winter, Faber & Faber, 1947

XX Poems, self-published, 1951

The Less Deceived, Marvell Press, 1955

The Whitsun Weddings, Faber & Faber, 1964

All What Jazz: A Record Diary 1961–8, Faber & Faber, 1970

High Windows, Faber & Faber, 1974

Required Writing: Miscellaneous Pieces 1955–82, Faber & Faber, 1983

Collected Poems, ed. Anthony Thwaite, Marvell Press and Faber & Faber, 1988

Selected Letters of Philip Larkin, 1940–1985, ed. Anthony Thwaite, Faber & Faber, 1992

Further Requirements: Interviews, Broadcasts, Statements and Reviews, 1952–1985, ed. Anthony Thwaite, Faber & Faber, 2001

Trouble at Willow Gables and Other Fictions, ed. James Booth, 2002

BOOKS ON PHILIP LARKIN

Michael Baron, ed., *Larkin With Poetry*, English Association, 1997

James Booth, *Philip Larkin: Writer*, Prentice Hall, 1992

— —, ed., *New Larkins for Old: Critical Essays*, Palgrave USA, 2002

Richard Bradford, *First Boredom Then Fear: The Life of Philip Larkin*, Peter Owen, 2005

Maeve Brennan, *The Philip Larkin I Knew*, Manchester University Press, 2002

Alan Brownjohn, *Philip Larkin,* Writers and their Work Series, Longman for the British Council, 1975

Linda Cookson and Bryan Loughrey, eds., *Critical Essays on Philip Larkin: The Poems,* Longman, 1989

Stephen Cooper, *Philip Larkin*, Sussex Academic Press, 2004

Roger Day, *Larkin,* Open University Press, 1987

George Hartley, ed., *Philip Larkin 1922–85: A Tribute,* Marvell Press, 1988

Laurence Lerner, *Philip Larkin*, Plymouth Northcote House Educational Publishers, 1997

Bruce K. Martin, *Philip Larkin*, Twayne University Press, 1978

Andrew Motion, *Philip Larkin*, Methuen (Contemporary Writers), 1982

— —, *Philip Larkin: A Writer's Life*, Faber & Faber, 1993

Stephen Regan, ed., *Philip Larkin*, Palgrave Macmillan New Casebooks, 1997

Janice Rossen, *Philip Larkin: His Life's Work*, University of Iowa Press, 1990

Dale Salwak, ed., *Philip Larkin: The Man and His Work*, University of Iowa Press, 1989

David Timms, *Philip Larkin,* Oliver and Boyd, 1973

alliteration the repetition of the same consonant or a sequence of vowels in a stretch of language, most often at the beginnings of words or on stressed syllables

allusion a passing reference in a work of literature to something outside the text; may include other works of literature, myth, historical facts or biographical detail

ambiguity the capacity of words and sentences to have double, multiple or uncertain meanings

assonance the use of the same vowel sound with different consonants or the same consonant with different vowel sounds in successive words or stressed syllables in a line of verse

bathos a ludicrous descent from the elevated treatment of a subject to the ordinary and commonplace

cliché a widely used expression which, through over-use, has lost impact and originality

colloquial the everyday speech used by people in informal situations

couplet a pair of rhymed lines of any **metre**

dactyl a metrical foot consisting of a stressed syllable followed by two unstressed syllables

diction an author's word choice

doggerel verse whose most important feature is a slavish adherence to a rigid and simplistic rhyme scheme and metre

end-stopped a line of verse the end of which coincides with the end of a sentence or clause

enjambment in poetry, when a sentence runs on from one line to the next, and even from one **stanza** to the next

free verse unrhymed verse without a metrical pattern

historicism a school of criticism that holds that literature cannot be properly understood outside of its historical context

hyperbole deliberate exaggeration, used for effect (from the Greek for 'throwing too far')

iambic pentameter a line of poetry consisting of five iambic feet (iambic consisting of a weak syllable followed by a strong one)

imagery descriptive language which uses images to make actions, objects and characters more vivid in the reader's mind. **Metaphors** and **similes** are examples of imagery

irony the humorous or sarcastic use of words to imply the opposite of what they normally mean; incongruity between what might be expected and what actually happens; the ill-timed arrival of an event that had been hoped for

metaphor a figure of speech in which a word or phrase is applied to an object, a character or an action which does not literally belong to it, in order to imply a resemblance and create an unusual or striking image in the reader's mind

metre the rhythmic arrangement of syllables in poetic verse

metrical foot a group of two or more syllables in which one of the syllables has the major stress. The basic unit of poetic rhythm

motif a recurring idea in a work, which is used to draw the reader's attention to a particular theme or topic

narrative a story, tale or any recital of events, and the manner in which it is told. First person narratives ('I') are told from the character's perspective and usually require the reader to judge carefully what is being said; second person narratives ('you') suggest the reader is part of the story; in third person narratives ('he, 'she', 'they') the narrator may be intrusive (continually commenting on the story), impersonal, or omniscient. More than one style of narrative may be used in a text. A narrative style is one that focuses on telling a story

narrator the voice telling the story or relating a sequence of events

ode a serious lyric poem celebrating a particular event or subject

omniscient narrator a narrator who uses the third person narrative and has a god-like knowledge of events and of the thoughts and feelings of the characters

oxymoron a figure of speech in which words with contradictory meanings are brought together for effect

onomatopoeia a technique which uses words that sound similar to the noises they describe, e.g. sizzle, cuckoo

persona(e) the use of an imagined character as the voice or speaker of a poem

personification the treatment or description of an object or an idea as human, with human attributes and feelings

post-colonialism a school of criticism focusing on Britain's role as a colonial power, and of its reaction to the loss of its Empire. Post-colonial Britain is Britain after the demise of the Empire

rhetorical devices figures of speech based on rhetoric – the art of persuasive speaking

rhetorical question question asked for dramatic effect rather than to obtain an answer

satire a type of literature in which folly, evil or topical issues are held up to scorn through ridicule, **irony** or exaggeration

sibilance the use of sounds with a hissing effect, e.g. *s* and *sh*

simile a figure of speech which compares two things using the words 'like' or 'as'

sonnet a poem of fourteen lines, usually in two parts, an octet and a sextet, with a definite rhyme scheme, normally in **iambic pentameter**

spondee a verse foot consisting of a pair of stressed syllables

stanza in a poem when lines of verse are grouped together into units these units are called stanzas. They usually follow a pattern with a fixed number of lines and a set number of **metrical feet** within each line

symbolism investing material objects with abstract powers and meanings greater than their own; allowing a complex idea to be represented by a single object

Symbolism an artistic and poetic movement based in France and Belgium and originating in the late nineteenth century. The focus was on spirituality, obscurity and **metaphor** as opposed to naturalism and realism

synecdoche making a part of something stand for the whole, or vice versa. For example, 'all hands on deck' where 'hands' signifies 'many workers'; or 'body blow' where 'body' signifies only one part of the body, i.e. the trunk

syntax the grammatical way in which words combine to create meaning

tetrameter metre consisting of four feet per line

trochees a verse foot consisting of a stressed syllable followed by an unstressed

vernacular common speech

Author of These Notes

Steve Eddy graduated from the University of Warwick with an honours degree in English and American Literature. He has taught English at secondary level and is the author of numerous English text books and GCSE and A Level literature study guides. These include guides to several Shakespeare plays, the Brontës, William Golding, Thomas Hardy, John Steinbeck and Mildred Taylor. He has also published a number of books on mythology.

GCSE

Maya Angelou
I Know Why the Caged Bird Sings

Jane Austen
Pride and Prejudice

Alan Ayckbourn
Absent Friends

Elizabeth Barrett Browning
Selected Poems

Robert Bolt
A Man for All Seasons

Harold Brighouse
Hobson's Choice

Charlotte Brontë
Jane Eyre

Emily Brontë
Wuthering Heights

Brian Clark
Whose Life is it Anyway?

Robert Cormier
Heroes

Shelagh Delaney
A Taste of Honey

Charles Dickens
David Copperfield
Great Expectations
Hard Times
Oliver Twist
Selected Stories

Roddy Doyle
Paddy Clarke Ha Ha Ha

George Eliot
Silas Marner
The Mill on the Floss

Anne Frank
The Diary of a Young Girl

William Golding
Lord of the Flies

Oliver Goldsmith
She Stoops to Conquer

Willis Hall
The Long and the Short and the Tall

Thomas Hardy
Far from the Madding Crowd
The Mayor of Casterbridge
Tess of the d'Urbervilles
The Withered Arm and other Wessex Tales

L. P. Hartley
The Go-Between

Seamus Heaney
Selected Poems

Susan Hill
I'm the King of the Castle

Barry Hines
A Kestrel for a Knave

Louise Lawrence
Children of the Dust

Harper Lee
To Kill a Mockingbird

Laurie Lee
Cider with Rosie

Arthur Miller
The Crucible
A View from the Bridge

Robert O'Brien
Z for Zachariah

Frank O'Connor
My Oedipus Complex and Other Stories

George Orwell
Animal Farm

J.B. Priestley
An Inspector Calls
When We Are Married

Willy Russell
Educating Rita
Our Day Out

J. D. Salinger
The Catcher in the Rye

William Shakespeare
Henry IV Part I
Henry V
Julius Caesar
Macbeth
The Merchant of Venice
A Midsummer Night's Dream
Much Ado About Nothing
Romeo and Juliet
The Tempest
Twelfth Night

George Bernard Shaw
Pygmalion

Mary Shelley
Frankenstein

R.C. Sherriff
Journey's End

Rukshana Smith
Salt on the snow

John Steinbeck
Of Mice and Men

Robert Louis Stevenson
Dr Jekyll and Mr Hyde

Jonathan Swift
Gulliver's Travels

Robert Swindells
Daz 4 Zoe

Mildred D. Taylor
Roll of Thunder, Hear My Cry

Mark Twain
Huckleberry Finn

James Watson
Talking in Whispers

Edith Wharton
Ethan Frome

William Wordsworth
Selected Poems

A Choice of Poets

Mystery Stories of the Nineteenth Century including The Signalman

Nineteenth Century Short Stories

Poetry of the First World War

Six Women Poets

For the AQA Anthology:

Duffy and Armitage & Pre-1914 Poetry

Heaney and Clarke & Pre-1914 Poetry

Poems from Different Cultures

Key Stage 3

William Shakespeare
Henry V
Macbeth
Much Ado About Nothing
Richard III
The Tempest

Margaret Atwood
Cat's Eye
The Handmaid's Tale

Jane Austen
Emma
Mansfield Park
Persuasion
Pride and Prejudice
Sense and Sensibility

William Blake
Songs of Innocence and of Experience

Charlotte Brontë
Jane Eyre
Villette

Emily Brontë
Wuthering Heights

Angela Carter
Nights at the Circus
Wise Children

Geoffrey Chaucer
The Franklin's Prologue and Tale
The Merchant's Prologue and Tale
The Miller's Prologue and Tale
The Prologue to the Canterbury Tales
The Wife of Bath's Prologue and Tale

Samuel Coleridge
Selected Poems

Joseph Conrad
Heart of Darkness

Daniel Defoe
Moll Flanders

Charles Dickens
Bleak House
Great Expectations
Hard Times

Emily Dickinson
Selected Poems

John Donne
Selected Poems

Carol Ann Duffy
Selected Poems
The World's Wife

George Eliot
Middlemarch
The Mill on the Floss

T. S. Eliot
Selected Poems
The Waste Land

F. Scott Fitzgerald
The Great Gatsby

John Ford
'Tis Pity She's a Whore

E. M. Forster
A Passage to India

Michael Frayn
Spies

Charles Frazier
Cold Mountain

Brian Friel
Making History
Translations

William Golding
The Spire

Thomas Hardy
Jude the Obscure
The Mayor of Casterbridge
The Return of the Native
Selected Poems
Tess of the d'Urbervilles

Seamus Heaney
Selected Poems from 'Opened Ground'

Nathaniel Hawthorne
The Scarlet Letter

Homer
The Iliad
The Odyssey

Aldous Huxley
Brave New World

Kazuo Ishiguro
The Remains of the Day

Ben Jonson
The Alchemist

James Joyce
Dubliners

John Keats
Selected Poems

Philip Larkin
High Windows
The Whitsun Weddings and Selected Poems

Christopher Marlowe
Doctor Faustus
Edward II

Ian McEwan
Atonement

Arthur Miller
All My Sons
Death of a Salesman

John Milton
Paradise Lost Books I & II

Toni Morrison
Beloved

George Orwell
Nineteen Eighty-Four

Sylvia Plath
Selected Poems

William Shakespeare
Antony and Cleopatra
As You Like It
Hamlet
Henry IV Part I
King Lear
Macbeth
Measure for Measure
The Merchant of Venice
A Midsummer Night's Dream
Much Ado About Nothing
Othello
Richard II
Richard III
Romeo and Juliet
The Taming of the Shrew
The Tempest
Twelfth Night
The Winter's Tale

Mary Shelley
Frankenstein

Richard Brinsley Sheridan
The School for Scandal

Bram Stoker
Dracula

Jonathan Swift
Gulliver's Travels and A Modest Proposal

Alfred Tennyson
Selected Poems

Alice Walker
The Color Purple

Oscar Wilde
The Importance of Being Earnest
A Woman of No Importance

Tennessee Williams
Cat on a Hot Tin Roof
The Glass Menagerie
A Streetcar Named Desire

Jeanette Winterson
Oranges Are Not the Only Fruit

John Webster
The Duchess of Malfi

Virginia Woolf
To the Lighthouse

William Wordsworth
The Prelude and Selected Poems

W. B. Yeats
Selected Poems